MESSAGE TO THE PEOPLE

The Course of African Philosophy

MESSAGE TO THE PEOPLE

The Course in African Philosophy

Tony Martin

The New Marcus Garvey Library, No. 7

Black Classic Press
Baltimore

Message to the People:
The Course in African Philosophy

Library of Congress Control Number: 2022932616

Print book ISBN: 978-1-57478-191-5
E-book ISBN: 978-1-57478-191-2

Printed by BCP Digital Printing
(www.bcpdigital.com) an affiliate company of
Black Classic Press Inc.
For a virtual tour of our publishing and printing facility visit:
https://www.c-span.org/video/?441322-2/tour-black-classic-press

Purchase Black Classic Press books from your favorite
Bookseller or online at: www.blackclassicbooks.com

For inquiries or to request a list of titles, write:
Black Classic Press
P.O. Box 13414
Baltimore, MD 21203

Tony Martin (1942-2013) was a preeminent authority on Marcus Garvey and the Universal Negro Improvement Association (UNIA). A native of Trinidad, Martin received his M.A. and Ph.D. from Michigan State University. He was tenured at Wellesley College where he taught for most of his career. He introduced a generation of students and others to Marcus Garvey. Martin's meticulous work solidified Garvey's importance to Pan-African history, the Civil Rights Movement, Black Power and African liberation movements around the world. Martin was one of the earliest scholars to view Garvey's legacy as a lasting testimony in the struggles of Black diasporic people. In 1983, Martin founded the Majority Press. He went on to author and publish other books on Garvey, Pan African culture, and several titles by other authors on related themes.

Black Classic Press is pleased to continue the legacy of Tony Martin by publishing selected titles authored by him and previously published by The Majority Press.

THE NEW MARCUS GARVEY LIBRARY

A Series of Original Works by Tony Martin

No. 1   *Literary Garveyism: Garvey, Black Arts and the Harlem Renaissance*

No. 2   *The Poetical Works of Marcus Garvey*

No. 3   *Marcus Garvey, Hero: A First Biography*

No. 4   *Amy Ashwood Garvey: Pan-Africanist, Feminist and Wife No. 1*

No. 5   *African Fundamentalism: A Literary Anthology of the Garvey Movement*

No. 6   *The Pan-African Connection: From Slavery to Garvey and Beyond*

No. 7   *Message to the People: The Course of African Philosophy (By Marcus Garvey, Ed. by Tony Martin)*

No. 8   *Race First: The Ideological and Organizational Struggles of Marcus Garvey and the Universal Negro Improvement Association*

No. 9   *The Philosophy and Opinions of Marcus Garvey (Ed. By Amy Jacques Garvey, Preface by Tony Martin)*

Contents

CHAS. L. JAMES
Commissioner of State
of Missouri

SARA R. ISAAC
Commissioner of State
of Pennsylvania

THERESA YOUNG
Commissioner of State
of Kentucky

ETHEL WADDELL
Commissioner of State
of Indiana

ELINOR WHITE
Commissioner of State
of Illinois

JAMES R. STEWART
Commissioner of State
of Ohio

NATHANIEL GRISSON
Commissioner of State
of Wisconsin

THOMAS W. HARVEY
Commissioner of State
of New York

Graduates of the School of African Philosophy, 1937

Foreword

Honourable Charles L. James
President-General,
Universal Negro Improvement Association

In keeping with the constitutional provision in the Aims and Objects of the Universal Negro Improvement Association, to establish schools and colleges for the racial education of our race, the Founder and First President-General of the U.N.I.A., Hon. Marcus Mosiah Garvey, made several attempts to educate some and reeducate others who would be charged with the responsibility of leadership in the U.N.I.A.

He sincerely felt that no one should be held responsible for his action unless he or she is educated or trained to perform those responsibilities, and since the U.N.I.A. had become the largest responsible movement in Racial History, its leadership should be thoroughly informed so that the proper information would be dispensed. Marcus Garvey was a man of vision, therefore his students had to be visionaries.

In every branch of the association, training departments were established. These included military training, training for nurses and programs for juveniles. We recall that under his direction a university was established at Claremont, Virginia in 1926. The Smallwood Corey Industrial Institute was renamed Universal Liberty University. Students came from various sections to enroll in this first venture. Your humble servant was one of the first trustees. The success or failure of this great educational attempt is a matter of history.

Many attempts were aborted but the idea lived on through forums, mass meetings, group discussions, lectures, books and pamphlets. Mr. Garvey's speeches were widely circulated for the racial education and culture of the people.

In 1937, after an extensive European tour and the establishment of the Parent-Body in London, England, the Founder called a Regional Conference at 355 College St., Toronto, Canada. At this conclave, he selected the following officers of divisions, who in his judgement were qualified to give him the nucleus of creating what he proudly named "THE SCHOOL OF AFRICAN PHILOSOPHY."

Students of the First Class were as follows:
Arthur Clement Moore, Toronto, Canada
Charles Llynell James, Gary, Indiana
James R. Stewart, Cleveland, Ohio
Thomas W. Harvey, Philadelphia, Pennsylvania
Nathaniel Grissom, Chicago, Illinois
Sarah Richardson Isaacs, Philadelphia,
    Pennsylvania
Ethel Waddel, Chicago, Illinois
Elinor White, Chicago, Illinois

Theresa E. Young, Cincinnati, Ohio
Abraham R. Roberts, Toronto, Canada

As the names were called, I had the qualification required but my ego told me that I had been an office boy in the Parent-Body, I had shined Mr. Garvey's shoes, I had travelled short distances with him, I had heard all of his speeches since 1923, I had attended all the conventions since that time, I had visited him in prison, and I had become the youngest vice-president of the famous New York Local with over 40,000 members. I had been appointed by him president of the Newark Division and state commissioner of New Jersey. And now as president of the Gary, Indiana division, I felt that I knew it all and that Mr. Garvey's time could be better spent on someone else. To my surprise I had the rudest awakening of my life.

Mr. Garvey shocked me. He said to me publicly, "James, you don't know. I know that you don't know because I have not taught you and you will take the Course of African Philosophy, so that when you say 'I know,' you will know that you know because you will have been taught by me." From then on, there was no question. I enlisted for the duration.

The class became one family. We ate together, roomed together, studied together, recognizing the professor as the chief architect of our intellectual destiny. As for me, it was a dose of humility mixed with the yearning for knowledge. For thirty days and nights, with two sessions per day, mass meetings at 8 o'clock p.m., studying until the early morning hours, we had no time for anything else but study, study, study. Then, finally, came graduation. Let the record show that I received the highest

grade. In every point of examination I was graded "E."
My classmates all agree that I was the leader of the first
class in the School of African Philosophy. We were
charged with guarding the written course with our lives.
The unwritten course was also to be engraved on the tablets of our memory. As I write this foreword, I am sorry
to announce that all my classmates of that first class have
joined with the Rt. Excellent Marcus Mosiah Garvey and
our other ancestors. With all our human frailties, I am
convinced that this first class has not failed our teacher
and that we have been a shining example to those who
come after us.

This course is ours. Whatever is written, distorted
and injected by unauthorized persons, using devices other
than the proper way that was given to us by the founder,
and applying the benefits to their own personal benefit,
please understand that "there is a destiny that makes us
brothers. None goes his way alone. All that we send into
the lives of others comes back into our own."

As the only surviving graduate of the first class, it is
important for me to protect the interest of those who preceded me into eternity and knowing that there are forces
that are trying to distort history, I hereby authorize Dr.
Tony Martin, who has been recognized and appointed the
authentic historian on the life and works of the Hon.
Marcus Garvey, by the Universal Negro Improvement
Association in convention, to publish the written document with the understanding that the right be preserved
for future generations, which is the charge of the Hon.
Marcus Garvey, Founder.

Let me hope that into whomsoever's hands these lessons fall, that they may use them wisely. For in these
lessons there is eternal life for Africans at home and

abroad, in that they testify to God's greatest gift to our Race, in the person of the Hon. Marcus Mosiah Garvey. Proclaim it to the world: "Africa for the Africans, at home and abroad."

Preface

The Course of African Philosophy is a unique document. With the exception of his poetical works, it is the closest thing to a book that Marcus Garvey ever wrote. Yet, forty-six years after his death, it is being published here for the first time. It represents, as it were, the last political will and testament of a man who stands without equal in the history of the worldwide mobilization of African peoples. For Marcus Garvey did not merely organize the most massive Black movement in the history of the United States of America. He also organized the largest and most successful movement among African peoples in the Caribbean area. In fact, as a serious Pan-Caribbean movement cutting across political and linguistic barriers, Garvey's Universal Negro Improvement Association (UNIA) has no serious challenger. Garvey's organization has an equally singular record in Africa, where it established itself, oblivious of political and linguistic barriers, in the European colonies of England, France, Belgium and Portugal, as well as in the independent state of Liberia and the racist state of South Africa.

In Central America, too, the UNIA spread with great rapidity from Mexico to Panama. In Canada it entrenched itself coast to coast, from British Columbia to Nova Scotia. Scattered Africa fell within Garvey's organizational genius in every far-flung corner, whether Brazil, Australia or Barry Dock, Wales.

Garvey lived from 1887 to 1940. His years of all-encompassing triumph coincided with his sojourn in the United States, from 1916 to 1927. His emigration to that country was, however, preceded by many long years of preparation for his life's work, long years of study, travel and organizational work, culminating in the founding of the Universal Negro Improvement Association in his Jamaican homeland in 1914.

After his expulsion from the United States in 1927, Garvey's organization underwent a long and slow decline, as the chief struggled to hold together his fragmenting colossus, from inadequate headquarters in Jamaica and later in England. It was in 1937, ten years after his deportation from the United States, two years after relocating to England and three years before his death that Garvey introduced his *Course of African Philosophy*. This was nothing less than a distillation of a lifetime of organizational experience. It contained a mixture of the techniques he himself had utilized to achieve success and an attempt to incorporate the hard lessons he had learned with the benefit of an unfortunate hindsight. Much of the Macchiavellian quality of the document comes from this latter consideration. Garvey had experienced, in a painful way, the treacherous potential enveloped within human nature. If he had his life to live over, he seemed to be saying, his would be a less trusting, a more cautious approach to people.

The immediate purpose of *The Course of African Philosophy* was to train a cadre of UNIA leaders who would carry on the great work of the organization after Garvey's death. Garvey designed the twenty-two lessons in London and took them to Canada where, from August 24th to 31st 1937 he conducted a regional conference for North American members of the Universal Negro Improvement Association.

Garvey's initial vehicle for imparting his accumulated experience was the School of African Philosophy, which met immediately after the conference. For most of the month of September 1937 Garvey trained a select group of UNIA organizers from the North American field. They spent twelve or more hours together every day. They listened to Garvey's lectures, ate together, did their homework together. During the course of the month each student was required to write out each lesson in his or her own handwriting.

The course, described by Garvey as "a most rigid system of training," covered over forty-two subjects. Much of it remained unwritten, for it was in the nature of a confidential in-house affair. Even the twenty-two written lessons reproduced here were guarded jealously from indiscriminate circulation.[1]

Garvey's overriding concern was to develop within his organizers a fierce Afro-centric view of the world. He accepted as given the fact that the white race had imposed its viewpoint on the world and he thought that African people would have to adopt similar strategies in their own behalf. The race first position would tolerate no permanent allies from among other groups. Whites were to be manipulated where possible, but their propaganda was to be avoided and counteracted. Under no circumstances were they to obtain positions of influence or control over Black organizations. The course, reported the *Boston Chronicle* after an interview with Garvey, would instill "an independent outlook, a philosophy entirely Negroid, void of anything that will subjugate the mind of the Negro."[2]

In the context of a confidential conclave, and with his lifetime of experience behind him, Garvey could be much less guarded in his speech than would have been the case otherwise. While forcefully attempting to lead his people out of the domination of the white group, he could accordingly frankly admire their methods. Whites knew exactly what they wanted and, in the final analysis, subordinated much else to their pursuit of racial self-interest. "Never swallow wholly what the white man writes or says without first critically analyzing it," he taught in Lesson 1. But this did not mean that the African race should eschew the white group's methods. "Things that may not be true," he suggested in the same lesson, "can be made so if you repeat them long and often enough. Therefore, always repeat statements that will give your race status and an advantage. That is how the white man has built up his system of superiority."

Garvey in his heyday had had to contend with white self-interest and opportunism from both right and left.[3] He simultaneously praised Lenin and Trotsky for their work in the Soviet Union and resisted the unprincipled attempts of the Communist Party of the U.S.A. to bore from within his organization. Here, in the *Course of African Philosophy*, he presented his students with a rare evaluation of Karl Marx. "[Communism]," he said, "was founded principally on the theory of Karl Marx, who knew very little about Negroes, and who thought and wrote less about them . . . . it seeks to put government in the hands of an ignorant white mass who have not been able to destroy their natural prejudices towards Negroes and other non-white people."

On the question of Jews, as on the question of Communists, Garvey's race first position led him to a duality of attitude. In traditional Afro-American vein he praised the Jews for their group solidarity and resented their positions of influence and power in certain economic and political aspects of Black life. He himself had come into business contact with Jews at various times, and with both good and bad results. He showed considerable pique during his trial for alleged mail fraud in 1923 where the presiding judge, Julian Mack, happened to be an important figure in North American Zionism.

For the most part there should be few surprises in these lessons for those already familiar with Garvey's ideology. What we find here is his standard fare of race first (whether in religion, literature, historical studies, intergroup relations or in any other area), self-reliance and nationhood. What is new and fascinating is the *tone* of many of these utterances, coming as they do near the end of his life and in a confidential setting.

Equally new in emphasis, though not in substance, is his insistent advocacy of discipline. Garvey emerges here, beneath the flamboyance usually associated with his name, beneath the genius for organizing, beneath the oratorical eloquence for which he was legendary, as an advocate of hard work, singleness of purpose and self-discipline. The leader must strive to master his shortcomings, he says. The race must strive for excellence—"The greatest men and women in the world burn the midnight lamp." Nor does he spare the lazy and unmotivated within his own group. Like a Booker T. Washington or a Malcolm X or an Elijah Muhammad, Garvey was not one to cover up the shortcomings of his own people. "The majority of the Negroes are ignorant," he says in Lesson 21. But the intent, as always, is positive. "As other people were willing to sacrifice their time and even their lives to christianize our race, so we must exercise patience and time to civilize our people."

Garvey cannot, any more than anybody else, escape totally from the confines of his time. There is much assorted homely advice on diet, grooming and love, among other things. Some of this is timeless, but some seems dated and passé, from the perspective of four decades later. The lessons are not without their unexpected asides of dry humour either. "Never try to make a speech on a hungry stomach," he warns. "You may faint and die before you are finished."

The first Course of African Philosophy was followed by examinations, held on September 23, 1937. Ten students were successful. They were Arthur C. Moore of Toronto, Charles L. James of Gary, Indiana, James R. Stewart of Cleveland, Ohio, Thomas W. Harvey of Philadelphia, Nathaniel Grissom of Chicago, Mrs. Sarah Richardson Isaacs[4] of Philadelphia, Mrs. Ethel Waddel of Chicago, Miss Theresa E. Young of Cincinnati, Mrs. Elinor White of Chicago and Abraham R. Roberts of Toronto. Joseph L. Gray of Charleston, Missouri "did not graduate but was continued as a student."[5]

This first group of graduates was immediately sent out as U.N.I.A. commissioners to the North American field. Some of them in due course instructed classes in the Course of African Philosophy. C.L. James taught the course in Gary, St. Louis and New Orleans. James Stewart offered the course in Cleveland.[6] Three of the ten—Stewart, Harvey and James—in turn occupied the organization's highest post, that of president-general.

In 1938 Garvey introduced the lessons as a correspondence course conducted from his London headquarters. His *Black Man* magazine published the names of seven graduates in its June 1939 number. Four were from the United States, with one each from Nigeria, Uganda and South Africa. They were Benjamin W. Jones of Philadelphia, J. O. Nwanolue of Onitsha, Nigeria, Mrs. H. T. McNairy of Detroit, D. S. Musoke of Kampala, Uganda, Mrs. Keturah Paul of New York City, H. Illitintro of Cape Province, South Africa and Mrs. E. M. Collins of New York City.[7] Names of additional graduates were promised for the next issue of the *Black Man*, but no further issues were published. Garvey died the following year, on June 10, 1940.

The School of African Philosophy came at the end of many years of U.N.I.A. efforts in the field of education. The organization's original aims and objects in 1914 included the establishment of educational institutions. Garvey's trip to the United States in 1916 was intended initially as a fundraising tour for the U.N.I.A.'s projected agricultural and industrial school in Jamaica. At various times during the 1920s the organization ran a Booker T. Washington University in Harlem, New York, a Liberty University in Claremont, Virginia and in-service courses for U.N.I.A. civil servants. Branches in several countries ran elementary and secondary schools. Famous educators and scholars such as Hubert H. Harrison, J. A. Rogers, Carter G. Woodson and many more were associated with the organization at one time or another.[8] U.N.I.A. schools had always had the same ultimate purpose, namely the presentation of an Afro-centric perspective.

The School of African Philosophy had itself been in the making from as early as 1934. In that year the U.N.I.A.'s Seventh International Convention of the Negro Peoples of the World, meeting in Kingston, Jamaica authorized the establishment of a "College . . . for the purpose of training leaders who are to supervise the work in different parts of the world."[9]

"Intelligence," said Garvey in the *Course of African Philosophy*, "rules the world and ignorance carries the burden." The intelligence of which he spoke was not merely book learning, but the self-interested common sense which the race seemed to lack. He expressed it this way in a fictitious father/son dialogue in 1935— "Education, boy, is a mighty force. It is the weapon of human control. If you can educate a people in the idea that you have, they will re-act to your satisfaction whether the education as a propaganda is right or wrong."[10]

It is fitting that the U.N.I.A.'s last educational endeavour in Garvey's lifetime should have been the first that he was himself able to conduct from start to finish. "I have given them all I know," he declared to the people of Detroit in 1937. "I am trying to make everyone a Marcus Garvey personified."[11]

Tony Martin
November 10, 1985
Wellesley, Massachusetts

Notes

1. Conversation with Hon. Charles L. James, President-General, U.N.I.A., September 1, 1985; *Black Man*, II, 8, December 1937, p. 4. Mr. James is the sole surviving member of the class of 1937.

2. *Boston Chronicle*, October 16, 1937.

3. I have documented this and other background information for this preface in *Race First: the Ideological and Organizational Struggles of Marcus Garvey and the Universal Negro Improvement Association* (Westport, Conn.: Greenwood Press, 1976).

4. Her name is sometimes rendered Sara R. Isaac.

5. *Black Man*, II, 8, December 1937, p. 4.

6. Conversation with Hon. Charles L. James, October 4, 1985.

7. *Black Man*, IV, 1, June 1939.

8. See, e.g., Tony Martin, *Literary Garveyism: Garvey, Black Arts and the Harlem Renaissance* (Dover, MA: The Majority Press, 1983) and "Carter G. Woodson and Marcus Garvey," in Tony Martin, *The Pan-African Connection* (Dover, MA: The Majority Press, 1983), pp. 101-110.

9. *Black Man*, I, 9, August-September 1935, p. 6.

10. Ibid, I, 11, Late December 1935, p. 16.
11. Ibid, II, 8, December 1937, p. 10. The speech was delivered in Canada. The audience was mainly from Detroit.

Lesson 1

Intelligence, Education, Universal Knowledge, and How to Get It

You must never stop learning. The world's greatest men and women were people who educated themselves outside of the university with all the knowledge that the university gives, [and] you have the opportunity of doing the same thing the university student does—read and study.

One must never stop reading. Read everything that you can read that is of standard knowledge. Don't waste time reading trashy literature. This is to say, don't pay any attention to the ten cents novels, wild west stories and cheap sentimental books, but where there is a good plot and a good story in the form of a novel, read it. It is necessary to read it for the purpose of getting information on human nature. The idea is that personal experience is not enough for a human to get all the useful knowledge of life, because the individual life is too short, so we must feed on the experience of others. The literature we read should include the biography and autobiography of men

1

and women who have accomplished greatness in their particular line. Whenever you can buy these books and own them and whilst you are reading them make pencil or pen notes of the striking sentences and paragraphs that you should like to remember, so that when you have to refer to the book for any thought that you would like to refresh your mind on, you will not have to read over the whole book.

You should also read the best poetry for inspiration. The standard poets have always been the most inspirational creators. From a good line of poetry, you may get the inspiration for the career of a life time. Many a great man and woman was first inspired by some attractive line or verse of poetry.

There are good poets and bad poets just like there are good novels and bad novels. Always select the best poets for your inspirational urge.

Read history incessantly until you master it. This means your own national history, the history of the world, social history, industrial history, and the history of the different sciences; but primarily, the history of man. If you do not know what went on before you came here and what is happening at the time you live, but away from you, you will not know the world and will be ignorant of the world and mankind.

You can only make the best out of life by knowing and understanding it. To know, you must fall back on the intelligence of others who came before you and have left their records behind.

To be able to read intelligently, you must first be able to master the language of your country. To do this, you must be well acquainted with its grammar and the science of it. Every six months you should read over again the science of the language that you speak, so as not to forget its rules. People judge you by your writing and your speech. If you write badly and incorrectly they become prejudiced towards your intelligence, and if you speak badly and incorrectly, those who hear you become disgusted and will not pay much attention to you but in their hearts laugh after you. A leader who is to teach men and present any fact of truth to man must first be learned in his subject.

Never write or speak on a subject you know nothing about, for there is always somebody who knows that particular subject to laugh at you or to ask you embarrassing questions that may make others laugh at you. You can know about any subject under the sun by reading about it. If you cannot buy the books outright and own them, go to your public circulating library in your district or town, so as to get the use of those books. You should do that as you may refer to them for information.

You should read at least four hours a day. The best time to read is in the evening after you have retired from your work and after you have rested and before sleeping hours, but do so before morning, so that during your sleeping hours what you have read may become subconscious, that is to say, planted in your memory. Never go to bed without doing some reading.

Never keep the constant company of anybody who doesn't know as much as you or [is] as educated as you, and from whom you cannot learn something or reciprocate your learning, especially, if that person is illiterate or ignorant because constant association with such a person will unconsciously cause you to drift into the peculiar culture or ignorance of that person. Always try to associate with people from whom you can learn something.

Contact with cultured persons and with books is the best companionship you can have and keep.

By reading good books you keep the company of the authors of the books or the subjects of the book when otherwise you could not meet them in the social contact of life. NEVER GO DOWN IN INTELLIGENCE to those who are below you, but if possible help to lift them up to you and always try to ascend to those who are above you and be their equal with the hope of being their master.

Continue always in the application of the things you desire educationally, culturally, or otherwise, and never give up until you reach the objective, and you can reach the objective if others have done so before you, proving by their doing it that it is possible.

In your desire to accomplish greatness, you must first decide in your own mind in what direction you desire to seek that greatness, and when you have so decided in your own mind work unceasingly towards it. The particular thing that you may want should be before you all the time, and whatsoever it takes to get it or make it possible should be undertaken. Use your faculties and persuasion to achieve all you set your mind on.

Try never to repeat yourself in any one discourse in saying the same thing over and over again except you are making new points, because repetition is tiresome and it annoys those who hear the repetition. Therefore, try to possess as much universal knowledge as possible through reading so as to be able to be free of repetition in trying to drive home a point.

No one is ever too old to learn. Therefore, you should take advantage of every educational facility. If you should hear of a great man or woman who is to lecture or speak in your town on any given subject and the person is an authority on the subject, always make time to go and hear him. This is what is meant by learning from others. You should learn the two sides to every story, so as to be able to properly debate a question and hold your ground with the side that you support. If you only know one side of a story, you cannot argue intelligently nor effectively. As for instance, to combat communism, you must know about it, otherwise people will take advantage of you and win a victory over your ignorance.

Anything that you are going to challenge, you must first know about it, so as to be able to defeat it. The moment you are ignorant about anything the person who has the intelligence of that thing will defeat you. Therefore, get knowledge, get it quickly, get it studiously, but get it anyway.

Knowledge is power. When you know a thing and can hold your ground on that thing and win over your opponents on that thing, those who hear you learn to have confidence in you and will trust your ability.

Never, therefore, attempt anything without being able to protect yourself on it, for every time you are defeated it takes away from your prestige and you are not as respected as before.

All the knowledge you want is in the world, and all that you have to do is to go seeking it and never stop until you have found it. You can find knowledge or the information about it in the public libraries, if it is not on your own bookshelf. Try to have a book and own it on every bit of knowledge you want. You may generally get these books at second hand book stores for sometimes one-fifth of the original value.

Always have a well equipped shelf of books. Nearly

all information about mankind is to be found in the Encyclopedia Britannica. This is an expensive set of books, but try to get them. Buy a complete edition for yourself, and keep it at your home, and whenever you are in doubt about anything, go to it and you will find it there.

The value of knowledge is to use it. It is not humanly possible that a person can retain all knowledge of the world, but if a person knows how to search for all the knowledge of the world, he will find it when he wants it.

A doctor or a lawyer although he passed his examination in college does not know all the laws and does not know all the techniques of medicine but he has the fundamental knowledge. When he wants a particular kind of knowledge, he goes to the medical books or law books and refers to the particular law or how to use the recipe of medicine. You must, therefore, know where to find your facts and use them as you want them. No one will know where you get them, but you will have the facts and by using the facts correctly they will think you a wonderful person, a great genius, and a trusted leader.

In reading it is not necessary or compulsory that you agree with everything you read. You must always use or apply your own reasoning to what you have read based upon what you already know as touching the facts on what you have read. Pass judgement on what you read based upon these facts. When I say facts I mean things that cannot be disputed. You may read thoughts that are old, and opinions that are old and have changed since they were written. You must always search to find out the latest facts on that particular subject and only when these facts are consistently maintained in what you read should you agree with them, otherwise you are entitled to your own opinion.

Always have up-to-date knowledge. You can gather this from the latest books and the latest periodicals, journals and newspapers. Read your daily newspaper everyday. Read a standard monthly journal every month, a standard weekly magazine every week, a standard quarterly magazine every quarter and by this you will find the new knowledge of the whole year in addition to the books you read, whose facts have not altered in that year. Don't keep old ideas, bury them as new ones come.

How to Read

Use every spare minute you have in reading. If you are going on a journey that would take you an hour, carry something with you to read for that hour, until you have reached the place. If you are sitting down waiting for somebody, have something in your pocket to read until the person comes. Don't waste time. Any time you think you have to waste put it in reading something. Carry with you a small pocket dictionary and study words while waiting or traveling, or a small pocket volume on some particular subject. Read through at least one book every week, separate and distinct from your newspapers and journals. It will mean that at the end of one year you will have ready fifty-two different subjects. After five years you will have read over two hundred and fifty books. You may be considered then a well read man or a well read woman and there will be a great difference between you and the person who has not read one book. You will be considered intelligent and the other person will be considered ignorant. You and that person therefore, will be living in two different worlds; one the world of ignorance and the other the world of intelligence. Never forget that intelligence rules the world and ignorance carries the burden. Therefore, remove yourself as far away from ignorance as possible and seek as much as possible to be intelligent.

Your language being English, you should study the English language thoroughly. To know the English language thoroughly you ought to be acquainted with Latin, because most of the English words are of Latin origin. It is also advisable that you know the French language because most of the books that you read in English carry Latin and French phrases and words. There is no use reading a page or a paragraph of a book or even a sentence without understanding it. If the paragraph has foreign words in it, go to the dictionary before you pass over the words if you don't know the meaning of the words. Never pass over a word without knowing its meaning. The dictionary and the books on word building that can be acquired from book sellers will help you greatly.

I know a boy who was ambitious to learn. He didn't have the opportunity of an early school education because he had to work ten hours a day. He was determined to learn, so he took to work with him every day a simplified grammar. He would read and memorize passages and the rules of grammar while at work.

After one year he was almost an expert in the grammar of his language. He knew the different parts of speech, he could paraphrase, analyse and construct sentences. He also took with him a pocket dictionary and he would write out twenty-five new words with their meanings every day and study these words and their meanings.

After one year he had a speaking vocabulary of more than three thousand words. He continued this for several years and when he became a man he had a vocabulary of over fifteen thousand words. He became an author because he could write in his language because he had command of the words. What he wrote was his experiences and he recorded his experiences in the best words of his language. At the same time he was not able to write properly and so he took with him to work what is called a copying book and he practiced the copying of letters until he was able to write a very good hand. He naturally became acquainted with literature and so he continued reading extensively. When he died he was one of the greatest scholars the world ever knew. Apply the story to yourself.

There is nothing in the world that you want that you cannot have so long as it is possible in nature and men have achieved it before. The greatest men and women in the world burn the midnight lamp. That is to say, when their neighbors and household are in bed, they are reading, studying and thinking. When they rise in the morning they are always ahead of their neighbors and their household in the thing that they were studying, reading and thinking of. A daily repetition of that will carry them daily ahead and above their neighbors and household. Practice this rule. It is wise to study a couple of subjects at a time. As for instance, a little geography, a little psychology, a little ethics, a little theology, a little philosophy, a little mathematics, a little science on which a sound academic education is built. By doing this, week after week, month after month, year after year, you will be so learned in the liberal arts as to be ready and fit for your place in the affairs of the world. If you know what others do not know they will want to hear you. You will then become invaluable in your community and to your country, because men and women will want to hear you and see you everywhere.

As stated before, books are one's best companions. Try to get them and keep them. A method of doing so is: Everytime you have ten cents or twenty-five cents or a dollar to spend foolishly, either on your friends or yourself, think how much more useful if that ten or twenty-five cents or dollar would be invested in a book and so invest it. It may be just the thing you have been looking for to give you a thought by which you may win the heart of the world. The ten cents, twenty-five cents or a dollar, therefore, may turn out to be an investment of worth to the extent of a million dollars. Never lend anybody the book that you want. You will never get it back. Never allow anybody to go to your bookshelf in your absence, because the very book that you may want most may be taken from the shelf and you may never be able to get one of that kind again.

If you have a library of your own, lock it when you are not at home. Spend most of your spare time in your library. If you have a radio keep it in your own library and use it exhaustively to listen to lectures, recitals, speeches and good music. You can learn a lot from the radio. You can be inspired a lot by good music. Good music carries the sentiment of harmony and you may think many a good thought out of listening to good music.

Read a chapter of the Bible every day; old and new testaments. The greatest wisdom of the age is to be found in the Scriptures. You can always quote from the Scriptures. It is the quickest way of winning approval.

Tragedy of White Injustice[1]

1. Read and study thoroughly the poem, "Tragedy of White Injustice" and apply its sentiment and statements in connection with the historic character and behavior of the white man. Know it so well as always to be able to be on guard against any professions of the white man in his suggested friendship for the Negro.

The poem exposes the white man's behavior in history and is intended to suggest distrust of him in every phase of life. Never allow it to get into the hands of a white man, if possible.

2. You can improve your English as you go along by reading critically the books of the language; that is to say, you must pay close attention to the construction of sentences and paragraphs as you see them in the books you read. Imitate the style.

Read with observation.
Never read carelessly and recklessly.

3. In reading books written by white authors of whatsoever kind, be aware of the fact that they are not written for your particular benefit or for the benefit of your race. They always write from their own point of view and only in the interest of their own race.

Never swallow wholly what the white man writes or says without first critically analyzing it and investigating it. The white man's trick is to deceive other people for his own benefit and profit.

Always be on your guard against him in whatsoever he does or says. Never take chances with him. His school books in the elementary and high schools, colleges and universities are all fixed up to suit his own purposes; to put him on top and to keep him on top of other people. Don't trust him. Beware! Beware!

You should study carefully the subject of ethnology. It is the subject that causes races to know the difference between one race and another.

Ethnic relationships are important for they reveal the characteristics of one people as different from another. There is no doubt that each race has different habits and manners of behavior. You must know them so as to be able to deal with them. There are books on this subject in the library. In your reading and searching for truth always try to get that which is particularly helpful to the Negro. Every thought that strikes you, see how it fits in with the Negro, and to what extent you can use it to his benefit or in his behalf. Your entire obsession must be to see things from the Negro's point of view; remembering always, that you are a Negro striving for Negro supremacy in every department of life, so that any truth you see or any facts you gather must be twisted to suit the Negro psychology of things.

The educational system of today hides the truth as far as the Negro is concerned. Therefore, you must searchingly scan everything you read, particularly history, to see what you can pick out for the good of the race. For instance, you will read that the Egyptians were a great people, the Carthaginians, Libyans, etc., but you will not be told that they were Black people or Negroes. Therefore, you should go beyond the mere statement of these events to discover the truth that will be creditable to your race. Therefore, in a case like that you would ask where did the Libyans, Carthaginians or Egyptians get their civilization from.

Following that kind of investigation you will come upon the truth that it was all original Negro and subsequently became Negroid. That is to say, subsequent people were mixed with other peoples' blood who were no doubt conquered by the Negro. As a fact, the original Egyptians were Black men and women, and so the Carthaginians and Libyans, but in the later centuries they became mixed in blood, just as the Blacks are being mixed in America and the West Indies by the infusion of white blood through the domination of the white man.

Never yield to any statement in history or a statement made by any individual, caring not how great, that the Negro was nobody in history. Even if you can not prove it, always claim that the Negro was great. Read everything you can get written by Negroes and their ancestry, going back six thousand years. There are statements in the Bible, in the old and new testaments, to show that Black was always an important color among the races of man. Abraham had company with a Black woman, even though he had his wife, Sarah, by whom he had Ishmael.

All the original Pharoahs were Black. Tutankamun, whose bones and body were dug up not very long ago at Luxor in Egypt, was a Black Pharoah. The Sphinx, in Egypt, which has stood through the millenniums, has black features. It is evident that as art it was portrayed to teach us of the greatness of men. When you are dealing with Jews let them know that they were once your slaves in Egypt, if you have to say so. There is [sic] good grounds for saying that civilization started in Africa and passed from and through Northern Africa into Southern Europe, from which the Greeks and Romans and the people of Asia Minor made good copies. The swarthy color of the Asiatics and the brunette color of the Southern Europeans are due to the fact that the cultured and civilized Blacks of Africa mixed their blood with them. Search all history and all literature and the Bible and find facts to support this argument and hold to it with a grip that will never loosen. Things that may not be true can be made so if you repeat them long and often enough. Therefore, always repeat statements that will give your race status and an advantage . That is how the white man has built up his system of superiority. He is always telling you he is superior and he has written history and literature to prove it. You must do the same. One of the great backgrounds for your argument which cannot be disputed is that you are older than any other man as a race because you are black. Your argument is that in nature everything by way of age darkens. Because you are darker than the rest of men, proves logically that you are older than the rest of men. Another proof of that is that even among white people they grow darker in skin as they grow older in age in a lifetime.

If one individual were to live for six thousand years he would surely not be white. If he were born white he would be as dark as the darkest of men. Therefore, the argument that the Black man is black because as man he is older than the other man is good. Use it everywhere you go to defeat the white man in his belief that you sprung from something else. Use the argument that the white man is white because most of the time when the Black man was great in Africa and had succeeded in running him across the Mediterranean into Southern Europe he had to hide himself in caves where there was very little light and air. He was almost covered up for most of the time in darkness. In natural creation, the child in the womb of the mother is almost white, even though it is a Black child, it is almost born white and doesn't change color until it comes in contact with light and air.

Living in caves for as many centuries, the white man, therefore, became colorless and the length of time made it so that he was born naturally white. You must interpret anthropology to suit yourself. The thing for you to do is to refute every pertinent statement of the white man that tends to degrade you and to elevate him. Turn the tables on him and search for all reasons in the world you can find to justify it. That is how new thoughts are given out by creation. Never yield to the statement of your inferiority.

In reading Christian literature and accepting the doctrine of Jesus Christ, lay special claim to your association with Jesus and the Son of God. Show that while the white and yellow worlds, that is to say, the worlds of Europe and Asia Minor, persecuted and crucified Jesus the Son of God, it was the Black Race through Simon, the Black Cyrenian, who befriended the Son of God and took up the cross and bore it alongside of Him, up to the heights of Calvary. Therefore, the Roman Catholics have no rightful claim to the cross, nor any other professing Christian, before the Negro makes his claim. The cross is the property of the Negro in his religion because it was he who bore it.

Never admit that Jesus Christ was a white man, otherwise, he could not be the Son of God, and the God to redeem all mankind. Jesus Christ had the blood of all races in his veins, and tracing the Jewish race back to Abraham and to Moses from which Jesus sprang through the line of Jesse, you will find Negro blood everywhere; therefore, Jesus had mostly Negro blood in him.

Read the genealogical tree of Jesus in the Bible and you will learn from where he sprang. It is a fact that the white man has borrowed his civilization from other peoples. The first civilization was the Negro's, Black people. The second civilization was the brown people's, Indians; the third civilization belonged to yellow people, the Chinese or Mongol's; the last civilization, up to the present, belongs to the white man. All civilization goes back to the Black man in the Nile Valley of Africa. Therefore, in your reading search for all these facts. Never stop reading and never stop until you find the proof of them.

You must pay great attention to sociology. Get the best books on the subject that you can and read them thoroughly. Find out the social relationship among other races so that you may know how to advise your people in their social behavior. Never admit that the Negro is more immoral than the white man, try to prove the contrary. Socially, the white man has debauched and debased all other races because of his dominant power. He is responsible for more illegitimacy among the races than any other race. He has left bastard children everywhere he has been. Therefore, he is not competent to say that he is socially and morally purer than any other race.

The mixed population among Negroes from slavery to the present, in certain countries, is due to the white man's immorality. Therefore, if you should hear anyone talking about moral depravity among Negroes and the moral excellence of the whites; draw the above facts to their attention.

When through reading and research you have discovered any new fact helpful to the dignity, prestige, character and accomplishment of the Negro, always make a noise about it. You should always keep with you a note book and fountain pen or indelible pencil and make a note in that book of anything you hear or see that you would like to remember. Always keep at home a larger note book in which you must transfer the thought or experience so that it will not be lost to your memory. At least once every three months read over that book and as the book becomes more voluminous with facts, read it over at least once a year.

By constantly reading these facts they will be planted in your subconscious mind and you will be able to use them without even knowing that you are doing so. By keeping your facts and your very important experiences on record, at the end of a full life you may have a volume of great value; such as Elbert Hubbard's Scrap Book. Get a copy of this book. It contains valuable inspiration. Always have a thought. Always make it a beautiful thought. The world is attracted to beauty, either in art or in expression. Therefore, try to read, think and speak beautiful things.

"Out of the night that covers me,
Black as the Pit from pole to pole,
I thank whatever Gods may be
For my unconquerable soul.

In the fell clutch of circumstance
I have not winced nor cried aloud,
Under the bludgeoning of chance
My head is bloody, but unbowed.

Beyond this place of wrath and tears
Looms but the horror of the Shade,

And yet the menace of the years
Finds, and shall find, me unafraid.

It matters not how straight the gate,
How charged with punishments the
    scroll,
I am the master of my fate;
I am the captain of my soul."

"Invictus,"
By W. E. Henley

Lesson 2

Leadership

To lead suggests that you must have followers. For others to follow you, you must be superior to them in the things that they must follow you for.

You must have superior ability in the particular. You must always be ahead by way of knowledge of all those you lead. The moment you fall down from the position of superior ability, you will automatically fail to lead and you will have to follow others. Therefore, you must be ever vigilant in keeping ahead of those you lead by getting the latest and most correct information for which they are searching, because for it they are following you. People only respect leaders and follow them, when there is something superior in them.

A leader must have personality; he must be clean cut in his appearance so as not to be criticized. An untidy leader is always a failure. He must be neatly dressed and his general appearance must be clean and presentable because people are supposed to follow him in his manner, behavior and his general conduct. A leader's hair should always be well kept; his teeth must also be in perfect order for people will criticize him for his unkempt hair, and his bad teeth.

Your shoes and other garments must also be clean. If you look ragged, people will not trust you. They will critically say, he has no clothing, his shoes are very poor, and it is logical that whatever money he gets hold of he will use it on himself rather than for the purpose for which he makes his appeal.

Never show your personal poverty to those you lead. They will never trust you. This does not mean that you should not reveal the poverty of the cause you represent, because that cause is your cause and the people's cause; in which both of you are interested. *Never tell lies* to those you lead; sooner or later they will find you out and then your career will come to an abrupt end. NO MAN EVER TRUSTS A PERSON A SECOND TIME whom he disbelieves once and has proof for his disbelief.

A leader, under all circumstances, must carry himself with dignity. He must not be a snob, but he must maintain his pride.

A leader cannot well afford to mix himself up with anything that is not dignified or self-respecting. If you have to do something that you know you will be morally and socially ashamed of if some one else knows; never do it, but if you have to do it, see to it that you are careful that no one else knows.

Don't carry your weakness on your face or in your eyes; somebody will detect it and you will be ruined. If you have personal weaknesses, try to conquer them and hide them as long as you can until you have conquered them; otherwise you will be ruined.

Every man can conquer his vices by bringing his subconscious will to play upon and against such vices. In everything you do, play the gentleman. Never be a hog, it doesn't pay. You lose a friend every time you play the hog. Keep smiling with the world even though your mother is dead. Smile with the world and the world will smile back at you; be vexed with the world and the world will be vexed with you. Nobody is obligated to you to make you happy, so don't carry your sorrow to the world and on your sleeves. Keep them to yourself and get out of them the best way you can. Leaders are not children, they must not, therefore, act as children.

Leaders must be self-possessed, confident, feeling self-reliant. When your followers see that self confidence they will believe in you and follow you. Always speak out right from your head and from your heart. If your heart is not in it, it is a lie. If your head is not in it, it is pure sentiment. Your heart and your head must work together. People observing you can always tell when you are sincere; that is, when you speak from your heart and your head. They can always tell when you are fooling them, by looking into your eyes and you cannot stand their gaze. At that time, indeed, you are lying. When your heart and your head is in it, your whole body expresses the truth and you can hold any man's stare.

A leader must not be extravagant, he must not be flashy in the sense of being over sporty. People will not think you serious. Always make your followers believe you are serious. You can be serious without being sour. Always think before you speak or act. Don't write or speak just to hear yourself. Speak or write only when you have something to say and never touch anything, by way of leadership, that you do not know about, because somebody who knows about it will have a joke at your expense. A leader must always have something to say, otherwise he forfeits his leadership and someone else who has something to say will supplant it.

A leader should always make an effort to be known in his community. He must acquaint himself with everything that is happening. He must know the governor of the state or country, the secretary of his state or his colonial secretary. He must know the mayor of his city, and all the members of the legislature. He must know the bishops of his city, the administrative heads of all government departments, all the preachers and doctors and lawyers and prominent business men.

Don't be seen with Communists too often; if you know them. Never take part in their meetings unless you are to make a speech against their principles and always see that it is known by the public that that is your only reason for going among them. Never let them call you comrade for others to hear; because you will be branded a Communist and your leadership will be destroyed.

You must seek to know all the people you want to be in your organization. Visit them in their homes, their work places, and anywhere you can meet them and always extend to them a glad hand. Always be diplomatic in your approach. If a Negro is in company with a white man, never talk to him about the U.N.I.A. If he is in company with some one you think is not in sympathy with the U.N.I.A., don't talk to him about the U.N.I.A., wait until he is alone. Never say anything to one person who may be in sympathy with the U.N.I.A. in the presence of two or three people unless you know that the others are also sympathetic; because when you are gone the others may try to undo the good relationship.

But when you meet Negro strangers, you may talk to all of them about the aims of the U.N.I.A. and try to win them over.

Never divide or create confusion between the different colors in the Negro race. Always try to prove that the standard Negro is the African and that all Negroes should be proud of their black blood, without insulting any color within the race. This is very, very important.

The idea of the U.N.I.A. is to unite into one race all the shades of color and build up a standard race. You should discourage intermarriage between white and Black and Blacks and other races. You should tell the people that it is an honor to be Black and that nothing is wrong with the black skin but bad conditions. Tell them that a well-kept Black woman or Black man is as good as a well-kept white man or woman. Never allow your followers to have their children play with white dolls because they will grow up to like white children and they will have them. Discourage the Negroes from having white pictures in their homes because those pictures will inspire them to become white in their ideas. Inspire them to have pictures of Negroes who have achieved greatness in their homes.

Tell Negro parents that they must teach their children Negro history, Negro pride and self-respect in their homes to counteract the elementary and high school education they get that holds up the superiority of the white race. Let the people know that God is not white nor is he Black; but God is a spirit and universal intelligence, of which each and every one is a part. All of us are a part of that intelligence.

No man can have the full intelligence of God; only partial intelligence. Therefore, no man can be God, neither the white man nor the Black man is God, they are particles of God. Let the people know that in them and in themselves only, is the power to rise. Let them know that God does not go out of his way to give people positions or jobs or to give them good conditions such as they desire. They must do that for themselves out of the fullness of nature that God has created for everybody. God does not build cities, towns, nations, homes, or factories. Men and women build them and all those who want them must work for themselves and pray to God to give them strength to do it.

Special Notes on
Intermarriage and Race Purity

For a rich Negro to marry a poor white is an unpardonable crime and sin; because it simply means the transference of the wealth of the race to another, and the ultimate loss of that wealth to the race. It is logically evident that if the Negro is rich, he gained all or most of his wealth from his race. Therefore, to ignore the opposite sex of his race and intermarry with another race is to commit a crime or sin for which he should never be pardoned by his race.

Teach the people to abhor such Negroes. Have nothing to do with them so long as they continue in that relationship. This must be done diplomatically, not to the hearing of the white race.

For safety, let the advice take the [form] of a whisper campaign; don't say it from the platform. Whisper it right through the neighborhood and never stop until the burden of your campaign is felt by the individuals; so as to teach them a good lesson that others may not do the same thing with impunity.

For a Negro man to marry someone who does not look like his mother or is not a member of his race is to insult his mother, nature and God, who made his father. The best tribute a race can pay to nature and God is to preserve its species; when it does otherwise, it is in rebellion. Don't be in rebellion against God, nature or your parents that you know of; they came before you and should have known better.

Insist on a campaign of race purity; that is, doing everything moral and social within the race. Close ranks against all other races. It is natural that it is a disgrace to mix your race with other races. To split up the race is unwholesome and does not tend to morally dignify the race. It will be a beautiful thing when we have a standard Negro Race.

In preaching race purity, be very careful because it is a delicate subject. Most of the people are ignorant of this idealism. You must never put color within the race against color. You must never insult any color within the race. Whatever has happened in the past was without our consent and truly because slavery and the wicked damnation of the white man imposed upon us moral behavior that we could not restrain. Now that we know better, it is for us to adjust these things within our own race.

Teach the people to respect all shades of their own race and never to have prejudice against anyone because he is black, brown, yellow or any shade that whites claim is not white.

Never allow any other race to preside over your affairs. If they come as visitors, they must conduct themselves as visitors. They must never have executive control over you in your affairs, because they will always say and do things to suit themselves and that are against your interest; even though they profess the greatest amount of friendship.

If they swear on the Bible, don't believe them. If they swear in God, don't believe them. Accept their friendship for all its worth to you and nothing more. Their interest as a race can never be yours, whether they be Europeans, Asiatics, Jews or whatever.

Never trust a Jew; don't let him know that. He is playing the odds against you all the time. He plays with loaded dice. His cards are marked. You can never win against him. Make this secret whispering propaganda in every community when you go into a Negro home. Whisper all the time that the Jew is bad. Flatter him as he flatters you and robs you. Never give him a square deal because he is never going to give you one. Tell him how much you love his people and how kind and nice his people are. Get all you can from him and give him nothing back except good words and pleasant smiles; this is his policy.

The policy of the Jew is; if he sees a Gentile dying on the pathway and a penny covers his eye, as a hope for recovery, he will take it off and let him die; he will not do this to a Jew. You have your answer to this. Treat him similarly. Always try to get something from the Jew because he has always robbed you and your fathers in that he believes he is the chosen of God and as such all other men must pay tribute to him. This is false and fictitious. It is Jewish propaganda. Ignore it and let him pay tribute to you; if tribute must be paid.

Lesson 3

Aims and Objects of the U.N.I.A.

1. To establish a universal confraternity among the race.

We mean by this that there must be a linking up of fraternal relationship with all the members of the Negro race to the exclusion of none.

Every Negro in the world must be a part of the confraternity. Every Negro's interest must come first in all the things of humanity. Not until you have served every Negro in the world should you seek to be kind to others. Charity begins at home.

The home of the Negro race is all over the world. You must attend to them first before you think of others. If you have a shilling or twenty-five cents to give away to charity, before you give it to other charities see that all other Negro charities are first attended to. So long as there is need in your race, attend to it first and always. Never deny help to your own race.

This is the meaning of confraternity. One for all and all for one. Never depart from this.

2. *To prompt the spirit of pride and love.*

It must be the mission of all Negroes to have pride in their race. To think of the race in the highest terms of human living. To think that God made the race perfect, that there is no one better than you; that you have all the elements of human perfection and as such you must love yourself.

Love yourself better than anybody else. All beauty is in you and not outside of you. God made you beautiful. Confine your affection to your own race and God will bless you and men will honor you.

Never be unkind to your race. Never curse your race. If anything is being done that is wrong by a member of your race, try to put him right. Don't condemn him without hearing him. Give him a chance to do what is right, before you denounce him. If he provokes you, try to put up with his ignorance and persuade him to be kind, good and gentle.

3. *To reclaim the fallen.*

Whenever a member of your race is down; pick him up. Whenever he wants genuine help and you can help him; do so. Never leave him stranded and friendless. If you cannot help him yourself, send him to someone of the race who can help him. Put an arm of protection around him and keep him from going wrong and feeling absolutely friendless.

4. *To administer and assist the needy.*

Let it be your highest purpose in life to assist the needy members of your race. Use all your influence in your country, state and town to help the needy elements of your race.

Seek government help for them. Seek philanthropic help for them. Seek help anywhere you can find it so that they may improve their condition.

5. *To assist in civilizing the backward tribes of Africa.*

Africa is the motherland of all Negroes. All Negroes were taken from Africa against their will and forced into slavery. Africa is the natural home of the race. One day all Negroes hope to look to Africa as the land of their vine and fig tree. Therefore, it is necessary to help the tribes that live in Africa to advance to a higher state of civilization. The white man is not conscientiously doing it; although he professes to do so. This is only his method of deceiving the world.

It is the Negro who must help the Negro. To help the African Negro to achieve civilization is to prepare him for his place in a new African state that will be the home of all Negroes.

6. *To assist in the development of independent Negro nations and communities.*

The Negro should develop every section of the communities in which he lives that is his, so that he may control that section or part of that community.

He should segregate himself residentially in that community so as to have political power, economic power and social power in that community.

If he scatters himself about the community, or if other people live in the community, he will be scattering his power and dividing it up with other people. If there are 10,000 Negroes in a town, they should live close to each other. If there are 500, 1,000, or 1,000,000 in a town, they will have the power of their numbers to do business, to appeal to the governor, and to voice their rights as citizens. In this respect segregation is good. To do otherwise is bad.

7. *To establish commissionaries or agencies in the principal countries and cities of the world for the representation and protection of all Negroes, irrespective of nationality.*

This means that there must be someone in every city whose business it will be to look after the interest of Negroes who may come into that city or country. His position will be like that of an ambassador, consul, or consular agent of a nation.

He will interest himself in all the things affecting the Negro race and see to it that no advantage or abuse is taken or made of a Negro who comes into the city or country.

He is to report all happenings affecting the Negro; and those happenings in which the Negro is interested, to the U.N.I.A. This will not be necessary where Negroes have a community of their own, but is applicable only to foreign countries, such as Europe, Asia, and South America, where the Negro may live in large numbers and have no contact with the government.

8. *To promote a conscientious spiritual worship among the native tribes of Africa.*

Considering that there are so many different religious thoughts, the Negro should be brought under the influence of one system of religion and the belief in one God. An honest effort should be made to instruct him in his particular desires and not to exploit him by teaching him different religions.

There is to be no speculative idea behind his religion.

9. *To establish universities, colleges, academies and schools for the racial education and culture of the people.*

This means that we are not to become satisfied with the educational system of the white man which has been devised by him for his own purpose; to lead others to obedience to his system.

The Negro must have an educational system of his own; based upon the history and tradition of his race. Therefore, the textbooks must be different than the white man's textbooks. The white man's books laud him and outrage the Negro. In such textbooks the Negro should substitute all that is bad affecting him for what is good relating to him.

Therefore, the Negro should not be satisfied with a college or university education from white schools. He should add to his schooling by going to his own schools and universities, where possible, or read such textbooks that have been adopted by his schools and colleges. These books should glorify the Negro; just as the white man's system glorifies the white man.

10. *To conduct a world-wide commercial and industrial intercourse for the good of the people.*

The economic life of the Negro is important. He lives by eating, wearing clothes, and living in a home. These are essential. To get these things he must work either with his hands or his brains.

The economic system lays down the fact that commerce and industry are the feeding factors in the economic life. Hence, it is absolutely necessary that the Negro builds an economic structure sufficiently strong enough to feed the arteries of his existence.

Therefore, the Negro should indulge in every kind of business that is necessary to earn profit; because it is by profit that he will be able to obtain life's necessities for himself and his race.

11. *To work for better conditions in all Negro communities.*

There should be a ceaseless effort among Negroes everywhere to improve their condition in every department of life and make their communities so prosperous as to compel the respect of their neighbor. No stone should be left unturned to advance from one stage of development and progress to another. There is always work to do in this respect.

Application

All the funds of the U.N.I.A. are supposed to be directed in these channels. The funds of the U.N.I.A. must be used for the race, and only the race. These funds belong to no one individual or group of individuals. They are held in trust for the race. All the profits made from investments in different companies that it controls must ultimately be used for the good and welfare of the Negro race at large.

U.N.I.A. property will be held in trust for the Negro race. Its wealth will be held in trust for the Negro race for serving generations yet unborn.

The U.N.I.A. shall go on eternally; with one generation handing it down to the next. No one person or persons can claim such wealth because it is for the race in perpetual existence. Stress this everywhere you go so that people may know that what they contribute to the U.N.I.A. is not loss to them. Let them know that their future generations may benefit from the gift they give today.

Black Nationalism

The culmination of all the efforts of the U.N.I.A. must end in Negro independent nationalism on the continent of Africa. That is to say, everything must contribute toward the final objective of having a powerful nation for the Negro race. Negro nationalism is necessary. It is political power and control.

No race is free until it has a strong nation of its own; its own system of government and its own order of society. Never give up this idea. Let no one persuade you against it. It is the only protection for your generation and your race. Hold on to the idea of an independent government and nation as long as other men have them.

Never be satisfied to always live under the government of other people because you will always be at their mercy. Visualize for yourself and your children and generations unborn, your own king, emperor, president, your own government officials and administrators, who look like you.

God never could have intended to make you look as you look and as you are, and make your king, president, emperor or ruler of a different race than you are.

This must not be a license for you to disobey the laws of kings of other races or rulers of other races, while you live under their control. You must always seek and work for a government absolutely your own, where you and your children will have a chance like anybody else in the state; to have a chance to rise from the lowest to the highest position; which you may not attain under other governments. While you are under alien governments get the best out of them as the rights of citizenship; but always have in view doing something to make it possible for your race to have a nation and a government of its own. Speak of this, dream of this, work unceasingly for this and never forget this, for this is the great task of the U.N.I.A.

Never confuse your ideas about Negro nationality with that of other peoples, so as to think that their nationality is good enough for you.

Never think that if Japan gains control of the world, they will treat you better than Anglo-Saxons or Latins.

Don't think that if the Chinese or Indians get control of the world your position will be better. All other races and nations will use you just the same; as slaves and underdogs.

Therefore, your only protection is to have your own government. Don't encourage Negroes to join Japanese, Chinese, Indian or any other movements; with the hope of getting greater freedom. They will never get it, because all peoples want all things for themselves.

Explain this thoroughly and sufficiently so as to discourage ignorant Negroes from thinking otherwise. You should teach Negroes to have pride in their own nationality and teach them not to try to wear garments that typify membership in other nationalities. It is ridiculous and people laugh at them for doing so. Teach Negroes to look for honor in their own race and from their own nation and to serve their own race and nation to get such honors.

Any honors they can get from any other race for serving that race they can get from their own for serving their race. Therefore, don't waste time in that. You can have your own king, emperor, pope, duke, your own everything. Therefore, don't bow down to other races for recognition.

When you have honored your own men and women, recognize that honor before the whole world to let the world know that you honored your own. If the world laughs at those you have honored; ask them if they want you to laugh at those they honored. What is good for the goose is good for the gander. If they laugh, laugh at them.

A white king has no more right to drive in a golden coach than your king and sovereign. Their pope has no more right to put on sacred robes than your pope. Their dukes and nobles have no more right to be dressed up in feathers than your dukes or nobles. Therefore, have pride in yourself and honor yourself.

Don't allow the other nations to get ahead of you in anything. Follow the idea of the Japanese. Every ship the other races build the Japanese build one. Every university the other races build for teaching men, the Japanese build one. Do the same. Always have your own because there will not be enough to accommodate you later on. Create your own.

Every Japanese you see is working for the good of his nation. Every white man you see is working for the good of his nation. Teach every Black man to work for the good of his nation. In conversation with him never leave him until you have persuaded him to this line of thought.

Go to all your lawyers, doctors, and ministers and talk this into them. Argue with them until they perspire confession. Go back again and again and talk until you get your man and let him work for a nation.

Always talk about a nation. Always feel that you see the nation. Use the object lessons of other nations to convince your people of the reality of a nation.

The sovereign of a people is in the nation. It is the result of a people forming a society of their own to govern themselves and to achieve their ends.

People with different outlooks and of different races never join together except they are subdued. They always find independent expression and action. The highest expression of this independence is in the sovereignty of a nation.

The flag of a nation is the emblem that signifies the existence of that nation. Have your flag. It is red, black and green. Be proud of it for it is the emblem of your race. When other nations exhibit theirs, exhibit yours. Make songs about your nation and sing them. Write poetry about your nation and read it; recite it. Glorify your nation in music and songs. Don't sing the songs of other races. Don't recite the inspirational poems of other races. Sing and recite your own.

Everything that inspires other races turn into your own tune and fit it to suit your own inspiration and idealism. See only yourself in everything. Make your nation the highest expression of human idealism. Then live up to it.

Lesson 4

Elocution

Elocution means to speak out. That is to say, if you have a tale to tell, tell it and tell it well.

The idea of speaking is to convey information to others. Therefore, you must speak so that they might hear you. You must speak with dignity, eloquence, clearness and distinctiveness. You must speak to be understood in the language you speak. You must carry emphasis when you speak.

To be a good elocutionist, you must embody in yourself clearness of thought, expression and action. First, you must feel what you speak and as you feel it, express it in like manner. If you feel the enthusiasm of a thing, express it with enthusiasm. Speech and truth should be just your feelings on all things. If you speak coldly or without emphasis it is because you feel coldly and not moved to action. Every man who is not tongue-tied by nature can speak. God gave him a voice for that purpose, therefore, if you have anything to say, say it out loud so that others may hear you.

In addressing a crowd of people in a small room you must raise your voice to reach the person farthest away from you in the room. If you are addressing one hundred people you should raise your voice loud enough in expressing yourself so that the person sitting farthest away from you will hear every word distinctly and in like manner, if you have an audience of one thousand, two thousand or five thousand. If you stand up on a platform in front of an audience of a thousand and address them in the voice you would use for an audience twelve feet by twelve feet, the people twelve feet away from you will not hear you and those farthest away from you will have to strain their ears to hear and understand you. They will become disgusted and walk out on you. When you have an audience you must make an effort for everyone in the audience to hear you distinctly. You must pronounce your words correctly for them to understand what you say. You must not run your words into each other. You must make your words clear and distinct. You must not rush your sentences but speak in short sentences that carry clear thoughts so that everyone will be able to follow and understand what you say. The idea of listening is to hear. When an audience doesn't hear every word of the speaker, the speaker has failed to make a complete impression upon his audience. Probably, the very thought he would like to leave is not sufficiently distinct and clear as to be heard, therefore, the speech is in vain.

Always speak in words that your audience understands. Never try to speak above your audience's head because it will be a waste of time. Nobody will understand you. The important thing in speaking is to be understood. First, always think of what you are going to say before you say it, otherwise, you will be regarded as a fool for talking nonsense.

In a speech, when you start a sentence always complete it. Never speak in long sentences because people cannot remember long sentences. When you are delivering a speech do so with emotion so that you feel what you are saying. Do not stand in one place like a mummy. People will think you are planted there. Put action behind your feelings and move as your feelings direct.

If you are honest in what you are saying, you will feel it and it will move you. Always be enthusiastic about your subject. The way to do that is to know it well. Make your hands, feet and eyes give expression to your thoughts. Never express what is supposed to be an inspirational thought without first giving expression to the thought. You can do that by the movement of your body according to the response of your own enthusiasm. You must hypnotize your audience by expression. Stare into their eyes and firmly express yourself. You must not shiver from their glare, you must make them shiver from yours. In that way you will subjugate them and make them do what you want. This is made possible by your honesty of purpose and confidence in yourself. If you are telling a lie you cannot subdue everybody or anybody who is looking straight at you, because they will see the lie in your eyes. If you have to tell a lie don't look at anyone. Your eyes will betray you. Whenever you see a speaker look away from the crowd into the ceiling or at the walls, he is usually telling a lie. A person who is always facing his audience is never afraid of the truth.

Speak forcefully always, particularly at the beginning, middle and end of your speech. Start off in a low tone. Then, five minutes afterwards raise your voice gradually until you have reached a convincing point in your speech; then you may rest by lowering your tone to raise it again to get renewed interest. Continue the same way until you are about to reach the end, then redouble your efforts to win everybody over to you on what you are speaking about. This is called your climax. Always sit down with emphasis after you have made your speech, then rise, again to do anything else, if you have more to do. Don't let the people believe that all your efforts were just to get a collection. If you lift the collection at the same time you make the speech they will think so; lift the collection immediately after the speech. If you made a good speech before, up to the end, they will listen to you; even making a speech about the collection. If the speech was no good you will have a no good collection.

To speak properly you must have good sound teeth. You must have clear nostrils. Your lungs must be sound. You must have a healthy chest. Your stomach must not be over full and you must not be hungry. Never try to make a speech on a hungry stomach. You may faint and die before you are finished. If you have a nasal obstruction go to the doctor and have it corrected. If you are suffering from lung trouble see the doctor. To be able to make a speech for an hour or an hour and a half or two hours, you must treat and train your constitution. Your chest is the most serious part to be affected. If you don't have a strong chest, you will feel exhausted in attempting to make a long speech. To prevent this, eat as many eggs as possible. You should eat eggs at least once a day, not hard but soft boiled or raw, if you can stand it. This will strengthen your chest and after a time it will become so hardened that you will speak five or six hours without feeling it. This must be done regularly and as long as you are going to indulge in public speaking you must eat eggs. You should also develop the disposition to drink water and sip it at intervals if your throat becomes thirsty and dry. It is the most difficult thing to speak with a dry throat. All the straining you do will be of no effect because your words will be monotonous. There will be no harmony and rhythm. Soften your palate with water and bring back the music to your voice. You must never speak in a monotonous tone. Speaking is really music in another way. You must strike the different notes, play the different notes and let the people hear the sound and the harmony. This is done by giving each word its proper note sound and emphasis. You must strike the right chord.

For goodness sake, always speak out. Always speak loud enough for others to hear you unless you have something to hide. The desire is to be heard, then let them hear you. Most preachers fail because their congregations do not hear them; especially Anglican Preachers. Negro Baptist Preachers and A.M.E. Preachers can raise more money than any other preachers, because they talk loud enough to be heard and have more emotion in their expressions than other preachers. This is a hint. Such preachers are always fat; because they always have responsive congregations due to their ability to reach the congregation in telling them what they want. If you want anything told, tell it and tell it well so that nobody will misunderstand. You must open your mouth and not be afraid of doing so unless you have only gums and are afraid of people seeing the nakedness of your mouth.

Always try to avoid a cold because it is ruinous to any speaker. Whenever you catch one and have to speak; go to the drug store immediately and secure some speakers' tablets to clear away the phlegm. It is good to use eucalyptus for inhaling to keep the nostrils clear so that you will have a perfect sound to your words. Don't chew your words, talk them out plainly, otherwise, no one will understand what you mean. Practice speaking to yourself in your room, in your own hall, drawing room or in any place where you will not be disturbed. Go to the sea, beach or the woods and talk to yourself or to nature to practice so that you will have command of your expression and you become accustomed to speaking. Never be afraid of your audience. If you know your subject well, you have no cause to be afraid. Always know your subject. Never make a long speech after ten o'clock at night. People will become restless and move away; because it is near bedtime. If you are called upon to speak at ten o'clock or after, take not more than fifteen minutes. If you are to speak somewhere, see to it that you are not called later than 9:30. At a certain hour of the night people are restless and tired and generally want to go home; they are never inclined to listen to speeches. Never apologize for any other speaker being better than you. Just rise to the occasion and try to beat the last man. Let the audience judge. If you confess that any speaker is better than you are, even though you are better, the audience may still give the credit to the other man, because you said so, by running down your own ability.

Always see that your clothing is properly arranged before you get on a platform; otherwise, people may see things to laugh at. Be careful not to make blunders in grammar, because people may laugh loudly and expose you to others who are not thinking. You should not make any mistake in pronouncing your words because that also invites amusement for certain people. If they remember nothing else, they may remember such mistakes and ever talk about them and create prejudice against you for it. So be careful.

When speaking you should always try to hold the people's interest in the best way you know. You may give a joke that is relevant or logical in emphasizing your point. Never give vulgar jokes. To be a good speaker or elocutionist is to hold a grand prize among men. If you can speak better than others you have a natural lead among them. Glory in this and strive after it. Remember, God gave you a mouth and a voice and you must use them for good results. Secure from any book seller, a copy of a good book on elocution and study it.

Lesson 5

God

There is a God and we believe in Him. He is not a person, nor a physical being. He is spirit and He is *Universal Intelligence*. Never deny that there is a God. God, being Universal Intelligence, created the universe out of that intelligence. It is intelligence that creates. Man is a part of the creation. So Universal Intelligence and man was [sic] created in the image and likeness of God, only by his intelligence. It is the intelligence of man that is like God; but man's intelligence is only a unitary particle of God's Universal Intelligence.

God, out of His Universal Intelligence, made matter and he made the mind. That matter is made by God, and man is matter as well as mind; therefore, man must be in the image of God, because nothing could exist without God. As God made the universe out of His universal knowledge or intelligence, so man in his unitary knowledge or intelligence can make a typewriter, an automobile or a chair, but he cannot make the universe, because his unitary intelligence is not as much or as great as Universal Intelligence. All the unitary intelligence of the universe goes to make God, who is the embodiment of all intelligence. So no man can be as great as God because he is only a unit of God and God is the whole.

Therefore, no man can measure God nor ask God questions, because he is not as intelligent as God, therefore, he cannot understand God. Therefore, it is presumptuous when man questions God from his limited unitary intelligence.

Man never dies. Nothing dies. Man is made of body and spirit. The spirit is God. It is intelligence. The body of man is matter. It changes from living matter in the man to other matter in the soil. It is always the same matter. It doesn't die in the sense of how we understand death. It changes. When man sleeps and passes away in the flesh he goes to earth that lives on, out of which, other men and things are formed. All matter is related, so man is related to the earth and the earth is related to man. We eat ourselves over and over again. When we eat the apple, the banana, the fig, the cherry, the grape; when we drink the water, we are eating and drinking ourselves over and over again. Nothing is lost and nothing dies. Do not be afraid of death, because, what you call death is only change and you are still in the universe either in the spirit of God to whom your spirit goes after the change or as matter, which goes on forever.

You are related to the flower, the beautiful rose, the trees, the fish and the other animals, just as you are related to God.

All of you sprung from God, who is Universal Intelligence. Do not be more cowardly than the rose, the apple, the cocoanut, the sheep, the fish or the cow, to do that which all must do, that which we call death; to die. If you weep, you are a coward. Die like a man, because

you are not lost. You are still there. You only weep
because you are a glutton, because you think that you
will not get anymore to eat and drink. You think that you
will not get anymore happy times. Just as you have been
feeding up on things and other beings who came here
before you, so someone else must feed on you to make
creation true; otherwise, God would not be fair to everybody and everything. God is fair and just to everybody.
He is no respecter of things or persons.

It is everlasting, as we know—
This thing we call Mysterious Life;
It had no beginning some say,
It's just a constant Moving Flow
It goes from this, then back to that,
And on it moves, in course well
     planned,
That circles universe and all,
Thus passing through each single lot.

Your life and mine is one long psalm,
In tune with that of other beings,
And everything that breathes the air,
In seasons rough and seasons calm;
One source they say contains the
     germ
That grows in range of Universe,
And all go back to this one Cause,
Whose life supplies the spreading
     germ.

By being part of Source Divine
Each life has functions strictly

drawn,
For all must bow to endless time,
In form and shape that mark each
    line;
So man must yield his flesh to dust,
With plants and weeds and birds and
    fish—
With rocks and mounts, and lilies
    too,
As trees break up in fibre crust.

Each one should like to hold his own,
And be a king in self alone,
But this IS NOT the way of LIFE,
That claims but one ALMIGHTY
    CROWN;
Thus disappointed, men grieve on,
For he should like his own strange
    way,
When suns and stars and steady
    moons
Would dance and change to suit his
    clan.

It's safer then to have one God,
Whose life is first and ever so.
And all the rest to live in Him,
With all the good they ever had,
For fleshy man would ruin things,
If he controlled the Source of life;
The day would see an endless change
From slaves who crawl to haughty
    kings.

Live on good God of timeless worth;
And keep man in his place to live
That when he rises to the height
He might perform his good on earth,
For life right here is sad today,
As lived by man in company,
If earth goes on, They grave should
    come,
To lead us all in goodness' way.

"The Everlasting Life"
By Marcus Garvey

Lesson 6

Christ

The doctrine of God carries with it the belief in the Father, Son and Holy Ghost. Christ is supposed to be the begotten Son of God. He had a special mission and that was to take on the form of man, to teach man how to lift himself back to God. For that reason Christ was born as man and came to the world.

If Christ as man never existed, but was only an assumption, it would have been a glorious assumption to set man a high spiritual example of how he should live.

There is no cause to doubt that Christ lived. Because you did not see him and feel him yourself as Thomas did, why should you doubt his existence. If you can doubt that, you may as well doubt that your great grandfather ever lived; because you never saw him nor touched him. Logically, there is fair assumption for you to believe that your grandfather whom you knew must have had a father in order to have been born. Logically, his father must have been your great grandfather.

You don't have to see everything to believe it. You must trust some things to those who lived before you. You have good reason to believe that somebody or something existed before you came here. Never doubt that Christ lived, never doubt that God lived because great things happened to prove that before you came into the world.

Deny that positively which you know of, and not that which you do not know of.

The New Testament reveals the life of Christ as an exemplary one. His life was faultless to a word. Therefore, it is evident, that he must have been a superior creature.

If he had played the devil and behaved like the devil, there would have been no example to lead us to the perfection of God. Because his life was perfect, is evidence and fair assumption that he was the begotten Son of God.

The greatest thing that Christ taught was love. Love thy neighbor as thyself; do unto others as you would have them do unto you. In these statements are wrapped the highest ideals of a Godhead; as in the relationship of a father with his children. There has been no greater philosophy in the history of mankind. Support this philosophy and never change until God manifest himself to the contrary, which is not likely.

It is evident that Christ had in his veins the blood of all mankind and belonged to no particular race. Christ was god in the perfect sense of his mind and soul. His spirit was truly God's spirit. His soul, which acted on the advice of God's spirit was never corrupt.

Christ's soul was the free-will thought that is similar to the soul free-will thought of all men. Whilst other men with their free-will souls become corrupt and do evil even under the guidance of the Holy Spirit of God, Christ with his free-will soul never disobeyed the Holy Spirit guide of God.

In every man there is the spirit of God, that is to say, that which is there to advise you and direct you to do good always. In each man also, is the free-will soul which is the mind. Each may accept the good guidance of the Holy Spirit or refuse to obey entirely.

Man generally disobeys the Holy Spirit of goodness and therefore becomes sinful. Christ never disobeyed the Holy Spirit of goodness, and that was why he was the Son of man with whom the spirit of God was well pleased because he lived a life so perfect as was intended when God made Adam and Eve.

The mission of Christ, therefore, was to redeem man from sin and place him back on the pinnacle of goodness as God intended when he made the first two creatures.

The life of Christ is intended to show man that by obedience he can lift himself to the highest soul expression in keeping with the Holy Spirit of God, of which he is a part, but only with free-will. A free-will can do as he likes. Man has a body, a soul which is his own identification of himself and the Holy Spirit of God.

In the vilest man, there is the Holy Spirit of God and that man cannot destroy the Holy Spirit of God because that spirit in him is the unit of God which cannot sin and cannot die because it is everlasting goodness.

The thing that sins in man is the man's individual soul, which is his mind. When man corrupts this mind or soul, he is called bad. He is in rebellion against the Holy Spirit of God that is in him.

When he dies, as we know it and call it death; whether he dies a bad man or a good man, the Holy Spirit never dies, it goes right back to God, the everlasting goodness.

It is the soul of the man which identifies him as a unit of creation. That passes away if it is bad and lives on like Christ if it is good. You can judge the truth of this philosophy from your own experience. Try to remember how you think if it is not a fact that sometimes there is something in you that tells you do this, and another something at the same time tells you do that. The Holy Spirit, which is goodness, is always telling you and advising you to do the right thing, but your free-will soul, which is mind, refuses to accept the instructions and advice of goodness.

There is always a debate with one's self to know what to do. You must analyze your system and your being so completely as to know when you are being advised by the Holy Spirit of goodness and follow that advice. If you can satisfactorily do that, then you can be like Christ and lift yourself to the highest plane of spirit and human life.

The Holy Ghost

The Holy Ghost is the spirit of God at large. It is everywhere. It is really what we call the spirit.

In everything that you see, there is the spirit of the Holy Ghost. Man can be a complete manifestation of that spirit, for as a unit in him the spirit becomes responsible and lives and acts.

The Holy Ghost is the perfect spirit of God's intelligence which is distinct from matter as particles of creation. No particle can exist in nature without the knowledge of God, because God created it. A particle may not contain the spirit of the Holy Ghost. When life is given and thought is to be expressed there we have the spirit of the Holy Ghost.

A bit of iron may not have the spirit of the Holy Ghost; but in man there are the elements of iron as well as other elements, and the complete thoughtfulness of man is made up of all of these elements which give existence to the spirit of the Holy Ghost, just as all things are related and man is related to all things in nature.

So God is everywhere in nature, but the spirit of the Holy Ghost is only in the higher thought life, and the highest thought life we know is man. The Holy Ghost spirit is always in man.

The DOCTRINE OF THE TRINITY OF GOD, THE FATHER, THE SON AND THE HOLY GHOST, is not commonly understood by the ordinary mind that will not think in the guiding spirit of God. To the mind that thinks with the spirit of God it is very pleasingly understood that the Godhead is one in three parts; all related and all doing good. You cannot separate them. This may be a mystery which the ordinary intelligence of man cannot explain because man is not God in intelligence, but nevertheless, it explains the riddle of the universe. It is preposterous for man to say that he can analyze God in his completeness because man is only a finite and small unit of Divine and Universal Intelligence. So while universal intelligence can analyze unitary intelligence, unitary intelligence cannot analyze universal intelligence.

So leave out trying to be like God by demanding from God in mental analysis; why he does what he does, and why he does not do the other thing. You are not competent. No part is greater than the whole. The whole is always greater than any single part and man is only a single part of God; so he cannot be as great in mind as God.

There is a confusion of expression between mind, soul and heart. These expressions are used with laxity. In fact, they all mean the same thing. The soul of man is the mind of man and when we speak of the heart, not the physical thing, but the expressive thing, we mean the soul, which is the mind. So always remember that you have a body, which is the physical case for the soul, which is the mind; which is the heart in the sentimental sense of the heart expressing itself.

The spirit is greater than all and it is the Holy Ghost and God in man. The spirit advises the soul. It guides and guards the soul and when it is disgusted with the behavior of the soul, it leaves the physical body and the physical body dies, as we describe it. In fact, the physical body does not die. It becomes matter in a different form. It may become earth again, from which flowers and vegetation grow and bloom, and from which man eats back himself in the form of fruit and vegetable life. Nothing is lost in nature and nothing really dies, because everything is God's that is eternal and everlasting.

A good soul may pass away in what we call death, like a bad soul, but that soul also has an everlasting identity that may pass into some higher realm of usefulness. It may become an angel or it may be used by God in some higher sphere.

The wicked soul never comes back. It goes out and that is man's hell. Its going out is called, "going to hell," because it never lives again as a soul. Therefore, a good soul lives forever. A bad soul passes out when the spirit of God has left the body in which the soul is found. The soul is judged before it completely disappears, and will recognize its punishment in the judgment before God. Then it is completely obliterated.

You can worship God by yourself. You are responsible to God by yourself. You have to live your own soul before God. Nobody, but you can save your soul. Others may advise you on how to shape your soul; because of your ignorance of life. Keep in communion with God. No one but you can save your soul; in your soul [lies] relationship with God. Therefore, always worship with your own heart, soul and mind when you want to commune with God. Make your heart, soul or mind your altar and express it in the following way.

My Altar

I've built a sacred place all mine,
To worship God, who is Divine,
I go there every day, in thought,
Right to my own, dear sacred
    heart—
        MY ALTAR.

No one can change me in my mood,
For I do live on God's sweet food,
He feeds me every day, with love,
While angels look at it above—
        MY ALTAR.

When all the world goes wrong
    without,
I never hold one single doubt,
For I do find a great relief,

When I do trust my own belief—
MY ALTAR.

I see the Saviour of the world,
Whose light to all has been unfurled,
He utters agonizing plea,
With shining eyes that surely see—
MY ALTAR.

I shall remain with faith of rock
To see the Shepherd lead his flock,
And when He comes to claim each
        heart,
My yield shall be in wholesome
        part—
MY ALTAR.

Man was redeemed by Christ to reach the perfect state as man, through his soul. The symbol of the Christ was the Cross in sentiment, therefore, man adores the Cross.

The Black man has a greater claim to the Cross than all other men. If it is a symbol of Christ's triumph, then the Negro should share in the triumph because Simon the Cyrenian bore the Cross. Simon the Cyrenian shared in the original triumph. The shortest prayer we may give to God, even if we never pray otherwise, is to make the sign of the cross, and say at the same time, "In the name of the Father, the Son and the Holy Ghost." It is a powerful prayer. It supersedes all others. If the words are repeated sincerely and earnestly from the heart, God answers that prayer. Do it always.

In going to bed you need not make a long prayer. Make the sign of the Cross and repeat the words the Catholics do. The Catholics appreciate the value of the Cross. That is why they make the sign of the Cross as a part of their religion. But they have no right to the Cross because they crucified Christ on the Cross.

The Cross is the heritage of the Black man. Don't give it up. This has nothing to do with the Roman Catholic religion. This is our religion and our interpretation of the significance of the Cross and Christ.

When it is said, "Thou shalt not kill," it is meant thou shall not kill the soul; because the soul is the personality of man. "Thou shall not kill," does not refer to the flesh because flesh is matter, and matter passes from one stage to another. By change, it is always matter, but if the soul does wickedness and evil, it dies. It only lives when it is perfect in keeping with God's goodness. Therefore, when it is said "Thou shall not kill," it means you must not kill the soul of man.

This is how warriors such as Napoleon, the Emperors, Pharoahs and the old religious warriors who fought battles among men interpreted it. This is how the Israelites interpreted it when they fought against the Philistines. This is how Joshua interpreted it when he fought against the Canaanites. This is how it shall ever be because man shall ever be at war with man in the fight of good against evil.

> Leaf after leaf drops off, flower after
> flower,
> Some in the chill, some in the
> warmer hour;
> Alive they flourish, and alive they

fall,
And Earth who nourished them
   receives them all.
Should we, her wiser sons, be less
   content
To sink into her lap when life is
   spent?

          "Leaf After Leaf Drops Off"
          By Walter Savage Landor

Lesson 7

Character

Men and women who want to be of use to themselves and humanity must have good character. Good character means the demonstration of the kind of behavior that meets the moral precepts of a civilization; the standard that is laid down by the society of the time in which you live and which forms a part of and guides that very character.

If you do not live up to those standards, in the highest sense, you will not be respected by that society. Your mission in the society for useful work will fall to pieces.

The greatest prop to character is honesty. Honesty is the best policy. Let no one believe that you are dishonest. If they believe you are dishonest, you are doomed. You will never be able to rise to a position of respect and trust except by some mere accident. You must live so clean that everybody can see the cleanliness of your life.

Never let people believe that you are a liar, but the contrary. Let them believe that you always speak the truth and live up to it.

Any conduct that your community or society condemns, be careful not to violate that rule or law, because you will lose the respect of your community.

Never borrow money, unless you intend to pay it back. Pay it back as quickly as you can. If you give excuses when you should be paying, those you are obligated to will think you are a trickster. Even though you subsequently pay them, they will be loath to trust you a second time. Even if you have to make sacrifices, pay your debts, because when you don't pay your debts, people talk about it and sooner or later everybody in the community knows about it and you are ruined.

It is a good policy to keep a good and honorable name. It is good credit. People will trust you on a good name. They will ask for the cash right on the spot and count it to the last farthing if your name is bad. People who trust you will almost take money from you without counting it. When you have lost that much confidence, you are a marked object and you may as well move from that town or city or community to start life afresh somewhere else where nobody knows you; where you may practice the higher principles and retrieve your name.

Never move into a nearby or adjoining community if you have lost your name. In the first place, go far away from it. No leader who is dishonest can hold his leadership. Nobody will follow him. Let your good character shine so that men will see it and talk about it.

Morality is upheld everywhere in civilization. Don't be immoral in your community. Somebody will tell on you and expose you; and the homes of the community will be closed against you and respectable people will shun you. If you have to be immoral because your nature is weak, then hide it. Keep it within closed doors and be sure nobody knows about it.

If you read good books and think loftily, you will not be immoral. If you are intelligent, you will not be immoral because immorality leads to disease, pain, suffering and ultimately to premature death.

An immoral person cannot find good company because no good person wants to take the chance with immorality. Those who cater to your immorality must be people who have no character and who have nothing to lose. They must be either sick or diseased themselves and therefore, don't care.

No respectable woman or man who cares about his or her future is going to be indiscriminate because that is taking chances. Therefore, when you find a person of immoral habits, it is someone who has lost all proportions of decency and health and doesn't care. Such a person is a social danger.

Sensible people do not give themselves away for nothing, but sick people and diseased people, like a drowning man, catch at a straw. Never be seen with those people in your community. Never be seen with a person of bad character. You will be roped in and even though your character is good, it will also suffer because of your association with that person.

If you have to keep company with the opposite sex, let your companionship be consistent and steady with one person. Don't run around always with different people of the opposite sex. This does not mean that you must not associate socially with all the people of your class. It means, if your name is to be linked up in the community as directly interested socially, let is be that one person, but don't run around with several.

As a leader, never flirt or indicate that you are a flirt. Never try to make love to two people in the same organization; where both attend and you are a member at the same time. A fight will ensue and scandal will spread and you will lose your reputation. If you have to speculate with your love, keep the parties far apart; at least in different communities, but not in the same town. It will leak out and be whispered about and you will be called a bad person.

Most of the deformities in a community are the result of immoral and loose people cutting loose. Sick people never produce good children. Disease in man is destructive. It destroys the species and wrecks the mind of man. The first thought a healthy man has of a poor minded man is that his parents were immoral and stamped their immorality on him, which he is to carry through the world by his particular affectation, be it in poor mentality or in [nervous] disability.

Don't be a public drunkard. Don't drink inordinately. You may contract disease by over drinking, and water your brain to that of deterioration. Don't take drugs or narcotics as a habit. They will have the same effect. Be temperate in everything you do. Learn self-control. By self-control, you can conquer every bad habit. You can do so by concentrating on the thought always that the habit is bad and will ruin you. Say to yourself, "I shall not be ruined. I shall conquer my bad habit." Say this and repeat it day after day until you conquer the habit. Let the habit be your opponent and then fight your opponent and beat it. Never give up until you conquer. If you follow this rule, you will beat down every bad habit.

Always see the injury that the bad habit will do you.

If you don't want that injury to your health, to your mind and body to bring pain, worry and unhappiness, then fight it to the death. This is what is called "man mastering himself."

Anything that is not good rise above it and be its master. Don't be a public nuisance. Don't go out in public untidy or poorly dressed. Always keep a good and clean personality.

Always bathe your skin and do so at least once a day. If it is not convenient, bathe at least three times a week. A dirty body emits bad odor and causes people to shun you. If you know you are dirty, you lose confidence in yourself. When you approach other people, you are afraid that they are going to find out that you are not clean. It makes you nervous and you lose your balance and sense of proportion.

When a man is clean in body, appearance and mind, he feels like a giant and a master. He is afraid of nothing. If he lacks these qualities, he cringes, bows and hides. He is never himself.

Don't eat like a hog, even in private. A custom or habit will develop on you and you will do it unconsciously. Observe good manners in eating and drinking when you go among company.

If you are invited to dine with friends and you are hungry, eat a little before you get to dinner, so as not to show how hungry you are. If you eat up everything, your host will talk about you when you are gone. He or she and the rest of their friends will talk about your gluttony and you may never be invited the second time.

Be courteous and gentlemanly everywhere. Be kind to and practice respect for all children. Develop the habit of playing with children and treating them decently. The news will spread. Children will tell their parents and the parents will get to love you.

Never abuse a woman in public. Never abuse a man in public. Never make a noise in your home. Never abuse your wife or your husband in public. Never make a fight where you are living or anywhere else in public.

If you are angry to the point of fighting, count ten and move off. If it is your wife, family, relatives or even friends, take your hat and go for a walk. Inhale the fresh air, look at the sky, landscape, flowers and stars and new thoughts will come into your mind. You will forget your anger. Go to your room, lock yourself in and take a book of poetry from your bookshelf and read the beautiful thoughts of the past. You may even read the Bible for consolation. Read the proverbs and the Psalms and you will come back to normal.

Never fall in love to the point of losing control of yourself. If you do, you will become somebody else's slave and that experience will surely take advantage of you and cause you to lose your best character.

Never love anybody for companionship, unless that person has the majority of the qualities that you like and appreciate. Never love a person more for his or her physical appearance or personality. First, investigate the character, disposition, temperament, behavior and thought of the person and when you find in that person, along with good physical appearance such as you like, all the qualities or as many of them as possible that would tend to satisfy you and make you happy through a lifetime, then love that person. But never love anyone better than yourself, because you are responsible to God for yourself. Only love God better than yourself.

Don't believe that anybody loves you honestly, in the

true sense of the word. Generally, it is something you have or something they can get from you as the reason why they love you or pretend to love you. When that something fails, you generally find that you were never loved; which is always too late. Don't put your absolute Divine trust in human love; because man is bad and is susceptible to change.

When you love one for the qualities you think that person possesses and those qualities are not fully developed, help that person to develop them for your own happiness.

It is better to wait to find the person with the majority of the qualities you like, than to rush into loving for a minimum of those qualities. As soon as you get over your passion, you will still be searching for those other qualities, and since that person does not have them, you will seek them elsewhere and break up your happiness.

It is best for people not to get married until they are about 30 or 35, by then they have enough time to see everything and understand everything. Don't try to get too many children. You will find it a burden and then your love will turn into slavery and unhappiness.

Never wear clothes as if you were sleeping in them. To do so, it makes a woman suspicious and it suggests untidiness to men. Never wear a dirty collar or a dirty pair of shoes. Keep your fingernails clean and your teeth clean. Take salts or purgatives at least twice a week to keep your system clean. It helps to give you clear thought and vision and it keeps your health in perfect state. A dirty breath is due to a foul stomach. People will shun you if your breath is dirty. You may notice people drawing away from the faces of other people when they are talking immediately before them. It is because such people have foul breath. It betrays you to the person and to all who are observing.

Sometimes by keeping a foul breath, tiny flies hover around your mouth and everybody knows that your breath is foul. A leader cannot be in that position; because when he is addressing the crowd, they will be visible objects telling the audience how foul his breath is.

Remember, a leader must be honest. You have your character to maintain. You can maintain it only by good conduct. Therefore, never try to fool anybody or deceive anybody.

Never fabricate nor falsify; if the thought should ever come to you, count the consequence and the risk. It may be your last chance, and it may be your first mistake. Most men suffer from their first mistake; from which they never recover.

In working for the U.N.I.A., prefer death to stealing from the U.N.I.A. If you steal from the U.N.I.A. hundreds of millions of people will concentrate on you when they find it out; you will be exposed if you are found out. They will have your picture before them to hate, despise, curse and to damn. Therefore, play honest with the U.N.I.A. and its principles, all the time, because you are dealing with the destiny of a race.

As you will not steal from the U.N.I.A., do not encourage anyone to steal. Do not shield anyone in stealing; expose him. Life is too short to reform a thief. If he steals once, he will steal again. Don't pardon him when he steals from the U.N.I.A. because we must speed up to get to the end.

To waste time to correct a thief is to hold up the program of the organization. Get him out of the way and march along.

Before you steal from the U.N.I.A., beg the U.N.I.A. Ask for help from the U.N.I.A., but never, never steal.

Never make love to another man's wife. There is always bound to be trouble. It creates scandal, which you will never be able to stop. It will ultimately ruin your reputation. Leave another man's wife alone. A woman should do the same. Leave another woman's husband alone. There has never been a case where doing such a thing has ever ended without a scandal. David was punished for it, and he nearly lost the Kingdom of God.

Lesson 8

The Social System

Society is an organization of mankind to safeguard and protect its own interest. When society is organized and is made evident by regulations, rules and laws, every member of that society must obey the said rules, regulations and laws.

Therefore, always live up to the organized system of society of which you form a part. The only alternative to this is rebellion. You should never join rebellious movements against society, except when there is good reason and justification for it.

Society is intended to maintain the greatest good for the greatest number, and that is always uppermost so that in thought you may have to reform. Any society must be calculated to bring about the greatest good for the greatest number and you must obey its laws, otherwise you are an evil genius living in the midst of that society and that society will seek to destroy you or compel you to obey its rules, regulations and laws.

You cannot live by yourself in a society. You must live upon the good will of your fellows. Therefore, in that society you must respect everything that tends to the good of all.

You should always seek to have something at stake in the community in which you live; property of some kind, so as to merit the regard and respect of the community. Society as it is organized into a community, counts first its worthwhile citizens before it thinks of others.

Property in a community is evidence of your status in the society of the community. If you have no property, have something of substantial value. The police, the officials and the government recognize property holders as the citizens of first claim in an organized society. They are generally recorded to be identified. Therefore, you must teach the people to own property and to be known and recognized members of the community.

Always adopt a friendly attitude towards the police in your community, because the police is that civil body of officials who are supposed to protect the citizens and see that their rights are not infringed upon. You should always welcome the police. The police are never the public enemy, but the public protector.

You should help the police to maintain order because if the community loses its peace, you will have riots and probably bloodshed. No peaceful citizen wants to be caught in such a dangerous state of public affairs.

Never join to incite public disorder. Keep away from it and be innocent to all that happens, by way of revolution. Never allow the U.N.I.A.'s name to be mentioned as among rioters; you will destroy the usefulness of the organization in that community and may cause suspicion to be cast upon it in other communities.

Always disavow any attempt to label the U.N.I.A. with riotous behavior. Whatever object is desired in a civilized community it can always be achieved by the approach of good reason and good judgment. Always use good reason and good judgment.

You are not in a community to overthrow the law in that community. You are there to live under the law. The national aspiration of the race is to find expression, not in revolution where you are established when you are under other people's government, but to accomplish the end in Africa. Therefore, never preach rebellion, because you will disrupt the society in which you live and it will crush you.

The highest service a citizen can refer to in a community or organized society is to maintain and preserve peace. When the peace is disturbed, it is likely that anybody may get hurt and sometimes most innocently.

Never join the mob. You will most likely be shot or injured even though you may only be curious. If you are shot or injured in a riotous demonstration it is almost [always] evidence against you that you were one of the rioters. So keep away.

When the riot act or martial law is read or proclaimed in your community, keep indoors. Give this advice to the people. Never join a mob in a foreign country under a foreign government, or where you have very little political influence.

Political Pull

Politics is the science of government that protects those human rights that are not protected by law. Law is already established. Politics add to the laws or change the laws. You should play politics to get good government.

The state, nation, or the community in which you live directly is always governed by politicians or statesmen. You should know them and become well acquainted with them for your own good. You need them in trouble and out of trouble.

Always try to know the mayor of your city and the government of your state, island or country. Try to know the other government officials also. To know them before you have trouble is to get help when you are in trouble; not to know them is to be at a disadvantage when you are brought before them. Always treat them courteously and friendly even if you don't mean it. Always let them believe you are friendly.

If you are to be a leader in your community this makes it even more imperative that you know everybody of political consequence, because you will have to approach them not only for yourself and for the organization but for the members of the race who look up to you as their leader.

You must never sell yourself to the politician. You must get around him in the most skillful manner. Get all your rights and the rights of others dependent upon you out of him without selling yourself to him, to keep him in office, especially if he is not a good man in the community.

Always make your vote count for bringing about the reforms you and others think are right for your community. Never exchange it for money. You should see that every citizen that has a vote does vote on an election day, especially when you have reforms to be enacted.

Whatever the conditions may be that give you suffrage, live up to those conditions to maintain and hold suffrage, because just at the time when your vote is most needed, may be the time when you are not qualified to vote because of your carelessness.

In countries where as a race, you are not allowed to vote, always work to get the vote, by way of reform. Use the help of everybody, but have political power to bring about the changes that will give you the vote. Otherwise, you will be governed without your consent.

To vote is to make the attempt to share in the government of the community. You should never be a political slave in a community, because others will take advantage of you.

Always cast your ballot for good government. Never support a corrupt government.

Approach to Government

Always make your government know about your presence. Never hide from the government. Whenever possible, seek an interview with the government on behalf of the people you lead.

Always impress upon the government that your movement is not to controvert the established order of the government, but that your people seek a homeland in Africa which is not to be achieved by revolution in the country in which you domicile as a citizen, but if possible, it is to be achieved with the co-operation of the government.

Leave all policies of an international character, affecting the organization, to the international officers. Don't complicate yourself with your government.

Constitutional political agitation is not a riot. If you are a citizen, you have the right of public assembly. You have the right to protest against anything that is politically wrong, but that does not suggest that you must riot, because good government always puts down riots. Good government always has a way to settle its political difficulties in the interest of society and the community of which you are a part, and of which you have a voice in.

When you riot against your government, you are rioting against yourself, because the government cannot exist without you. That is why there is a constitution. When the constitution is insufficient to give you all the protection you need, change it by political action. Vote for change, do not riot for change.

Lesson 9

Diplomacy

Diplomacy is a word used to express the peculiar relationship between nations. Diplomacy is the relationship that nations use to conduct their communications or approach in dealing with matters of state and to affect the relationship of a certain nature between them. In the broader sense, diplomacy means the thoughtful and careful consideration of words and ideas expressed to reduce the words and ideas to the level of being the least offensive, while they carry the force of what is desired to the maximum.

To be a diplomat, one has to be very careful in his expressions before indulging in them. He must think seriously and calculatingly so that his thoughts and words may have the desired effect without arousing suspicion or inviting hostility. You must first be a very skillful thinker and psychologist to be a diplomat. A diplomat never reveals his true state of mind. He never reveals his hand in dealing with a situation. He always keeps a line of defense for whatever he says or does in reserve.

A diplomat never talks before he thinks. He thinks an idea over several times before he expresses it. The idea is that he must not be found wanting or on the wrong side of any question. If he is found on the wrong side, his efforts at diplomacy fail. He must be able to read other peoples' minds and intentions and use that knowledge to safeguard and protect himself and the interest he represents.

A skillful diplomat is always master of the situation. He is able to fool or deceive others to gain his point. He never exposes himself to be taken advantage of. He always leaves a loophole for escape from danger or trouble. His language is always couched in a manner to carry weight in the particular direction, but at the same time not to be so offensive or revealing as to cause the person dealt with to immediately jump at conclusions by the completeness of the thought expressed. In fact, a diplomat always gives out expressions that carry double meanings; or more than double meanings, so that if one interpretation is dangerous to effecting a good relationship, he can always fall back and say it was not intended that way.

In diplomacy, if you mean to take advantage of the other person, never open a suggestion, but gauge your words most carefully to ultimately win that in view [sic], without expressing it in the raw.

A good way to get good results is to actually feed your opponent with good words that mean nothing and then when you come down to the business part, hold your ground, but still use good and pleasant words to win.

Never approach anybody that you want to get anything out of or any good results from, in an offensive manner; to the contrary, win them with the perfect smile in the most gentle manner. Do this even with your enemy, until your enemy has positively delivered himself and there is no other alternative; then show your hand. Never show your hand at the start. The idea is to make friends and to get results, rather than make enemies and lose results. This must be applied to all phases of organization work dealing with the race and dealing with others of other races.

It is said that a kind word turneth away wrath. It is good diplomacy. Even if a man is going to kill you by threatening you; it is best to smile with him before he actually carries out the intention, so as to prevent him from doing so by showing him a smile rather than to suggest the gravity of your indignation which will cause him to think that you are going to kill him first; then he will surely kill you in self-defense, even though he first threatened you. Many a man have been killed when their assailant did not really mean to kill them, but only to bluff them; but in taking the matter too seriously and showing that he was going to do some killing too, he gets killed by the man protecting himself after his threat, to keep from being killed.

Never lose your head in dealing with a problem because in doing so you are bound to blunder and ultimately lose. Even if you are in an accident where you come face to face with death, don't lose your head, because you may need your calm and collective judgement to save your life. The moment you lose your head, you are taking chances. The odds are against you.

Morally, a diplomat must be a scamp; in that he must be a mental twister. He cannot deal with affairs with a clean conscience because he is to anticipate the evil of other men's designs, because the world and mankind are immoral and dishonest in their behavior. He necessarily has to adopt such a method as to safeguard himself or his interest from such designs.

You cannot be a true Christian before the act, but become so afterwards by repentance, which is personal. If you are protecting the interest of others, you have to sink your own personality, but still recognize the fact that you are responsible to those others. Therefore, you have to adopt all the methods of diplomacy to protect others, hence, you cannot do so with a very Christian soul because most of the souls you are dealing with are corrupt.

After you have dealt with them and you have won your point; if there was any act that was immoral or crooked which enabled you to win your point, then pray afterwards for forgiveness, but not before. Be sure that the act is done and leave the act where it is; if it is in the interest of others, then square your conscience with God.

If the truth is going to affect your cause then never speak of it, but go around it in every kind of ambiguous way to justify your lie to save the cause. If you have won your cause by a lie, then as early as possible try to make the cause right; but only after you have won, for no cause can continue successfully without righteousness of the thing from all your imaginative experience.

Never give up in seeking support. If one logic fails, use another until you have talked out your opponent by semblance of justification. You may say, "I don't mean so and so. It was not the way I intended it; I have a different idea entirely, you are misunderstanding me, you have a misconception of what I mean; you probably didn't hear me when I said so and so, I may admit that I was not clear enough, but I didn't mean what you say." Then be able to build up a new argument on that and let the thing that you are arguing about take a back seat, so that they will forget what you were arguing about and take you up on the other things you have said, and make that the debate. Thereby, you leave the situation where it was for another time.

Always try to lead the other fellow away from the true idea. If you are on the wrong side, build up a new argument and hold him on that until you have worn him out. Let him say that is not the argument, then still persist in something else.

Always profess friendship for your enemy so as to disarm him. Don't refer to him as Mr. Brown. Say, "My good friend Mr. Brown." "I cannot understand why my good friend is so opposed to me, I have always thought of him as a kindly disposed man and a very good fellow." But always watch him, don't take any chances.

Offer your enemy gifts that you can afford to lose; so as to win him like the Greeks bringing gifts. Your words must be formed and positive when you want to commit other people. For instance, "Do you intend to pay my money?" "Have you made up your mind to answer my letter?" Always let it be a question that can be answered with a *yes* or *no*.

Don't suggest to anybody in long sentences. When you ought to commit yourself, do so in veiled language and never finally commit yourself until you are ready to close the matter. Always try to escape giving yes or no to any question that is important. If you have to say yes or no, do so in long explanations, so that you may escape out of the explanation from the positive answer. If trouble is involved, it becomes your defense. Always try to leave in your remark or words room for controversy or denial of meaning as decided on by the other party.

When you want to protect yourself and trap the other fellow, let him write you short sentences by leading him up to such a manner of reply. When you have to answer, make your sentences long and capable of taking many interpretations. If you want to close the matter directly to your interest, then clinch it by accepting his argument in short sentences that cannot be misunderstood in law or arbitration.

When you are inviting explanations, make your sentences very short and to the point. When you are asked to give explanations, consider carefully if you should make your sentences long or short. Use discretion.

Always allow the other fellow to talk first by leading him. Let him talk of everything in his manner, so that you may know your man. Never let him lead you out. Always be reserved; in a word, be a good listener. Then when you have everything on the other fellow, decide the situation and take action.

To get a man to talk, offer him courtesy. Offer him a drink, a cigar, etc. Say, "It is a beautiful day, isn't it?" "How have you been doing lately?" "Are you comfortable where you live?" "What do you think of so and so?" If he is reticent, you know you have a hard customer to deal with. Then find out his weakness by investigation and when you find it, invite him back again and cater to that weakness.

His weakness may be for ladies. Invite him to meet your best friend and get your friend to pump him and tell you what you could not get from him yourself. If you are dealing with the opposite sex, do the same thing. If he is addicted to drinking, give him a few extra drinks and let him talk, but you must not drink as much as he, otherwise you will be in the same position. Use your skill in letting him believe that you are drinking too; but don't drink.

If you cannot get him by himself, get his friend to tell you all he knows about him. If the knowledge possessed by the person is important to you, never stop following him, even if you have to go 6,000 miles, directly or indirectly, to get your information. You may get it through an agent, a neighbor of his or a person he does business with. Follow every clue of an association until you get your information about the subject.

Never accept invitations from your enemies. Always find some excuse with kind thanks. If you have once injured a man, never trust him completely, because he is always waiting for his chance to get even with you.

Never talk your personal business or the business of your cause to a stranger. Tell him nothing until you know him sufficiently.

Don't accept complete friendship on first approach. Carefully find out if he or she is worthy of being a good and true friend. Otherwise, you may find yourself in the ditch.

Never give valuable papers or anything of value to a first acquaintance or a cordial friend or neighbor to keep. If the documents are very valuable, by way of information, don't allow even members of your own household to keep them. Keep them secretly and privately because you don't know who may give you away; even innocently. There is always a *third person* in everybody's life. *Be careful of that third person.* That person may come between a man and his wife, a brother and his brother, a sister and her sister, a father and his children, a mother and her children. *Remember, there is always a third person and that third person may not like you very much.*

Also be careful of the second person, because the third person always comes in through the second person.

You may quarrel with the second person, sometimes, and in the passion of revenge; which you may regret afterwards, the second person may reveal your secrets. Therefore, take your secrets to the grave and only let God know about them.

Never lose your head and divulge anything that would mean trouble for you with the law. The person who has the secret may change his mind about you, and turn you in; even after twenty years.

Many people get into trouble without knowing where the trouble comes from. Sometimes it comes right from your own home, by talking too much in your own home and by the circles in your home not appreciating your position. They innocently give the information out to other parties who are not interested in you, but are probably interested in seeing that the one you have offended gets justice. Therefore, the person prefers to see you hanged, rather than see his friend, whom you have injured go without justice because of what you might have done to that person in your secret.

Lesson 10

Economy

There are several kinds of economy, but this subject deals specifically with financial economy.

Economy is based upon good and sane judgement. The practice of it is that you must always be on the safe side of your bargains or your dealings. Never exhaust yourself, always have a reserve.

There should always be something left over that you may fall back on in time of need. Money is the prop of life; in that it pays for all necessities and offers security for all opportunities. In earning money, one should never spend as much money as he earns. That is bad business.

Whatever his earning capacity, he should always be thrifty enough to save at least 15 to 20% of his income, storing it up for making better opportunities when they come and providing for a rainy day.

If you spend all you earn, you are on the edge of bankruptcy all the time. If you spend more than you earn, you are not only a fool, but you are a very dishonest person, and you are bound to suffer without any other chance. Therefore, always make it a policy to save money out of your earnings, never mind how small it is.

If you have better commercial ideas than your present job calls for and your present remuneration warrants, then save out of your present earnings to take advantage of the opportunity to improve yourself within a reasonable time in achieving these ideas.

Never engage yourself in living luxuriously when you can only live ordinarily. Ultimately, you are bound to fail and be the laughing stock of your friends in the community by not being able to keep up your luxurious standard of living on a limited purse.

Never buy anything for more money than you have or positively expect to have within the time limited for the purchase.

Never give away money that you cannot spare. Never give away anything of value that can be turned into money except you can spare it.

Never borrow on interest from anybody. If you can, within a reasonable time pay your debts. If you pay your own debts with your own money, you will save the interest for yourself that you pay to others. The moment you start paying interest to others on money borrowed you become a slave working for somebody else. It is better to wait until you have the money yourself to do a thing before you borrow it to purchase that thing and pay interest on it.

At the same time, you must use good judgment to find out whether it is to your advantage to seek an opportunity of doing something big with somebody else's money, even with interest to be paid. You must decide if that particular business will positively bring enough to meet the interest and give you sufficient profit to justify the risk you take in assuming the responsibility of paying interest to others may be of value [sic].

The moment you are loaned money on interest to do anything, the person loaning you the money must be credited as being wise enough to know before hand if more money can be made out of the thing or investment than only the interest. If it is so, it is likely that he himself will go into that business and not give you the chance to go into it with his money. He may be a friend and want to help you, but few money lenders are friends. They are lending for usury and have no souls. At least their souls are bad. So be careful in borrowing money to go into business.

It is better you save and wait until you are able to go into business on your own account before you take the risk. It is bad business to go into any business without enough capital to run that business . . . 99 cases out of 100 will fail.

Always consider cost before you go into anything and in figuring out the cost be sure that there is a margin of profit before you do the thing; otherwise it is not worth while doing.

If you are going to address a meeting 100 miles away, first count the cost of railroad fare or transportation to and from, the cost of the meeting, your living expenses while going and staying at the meeting and returning from the meeting; the percentage to pay those who are looking after the meeting and the prospect of getting a crowd large enough that will meet all these expenses and leave you with a profit of at least 25%.

If there is no profit in it, you are taking a risk and when you are finished you will be sorry you went.

Always work out before hand the possible financial results of every transaction and be sure that your arrangements are of such as to bring profit at the end; otherwise you are wasting time.

As far as the U.N.I.A. is concerned, you should always calculate for profit for the association in everything you do. Profit comes in many ways to the association. For instance, if you go to address a meeting 100 miles away, profit will come by new members joining the association, the establishing of agencies there, for the association; leaving behind the sentiments of the association may be an advantage to any money you receive for the expenses of the meeting. As long as you have converted and attached someone permanently to the U.N.I.A.; that may be considered as profit.

Always seek to get some profit, otherwise your work is a failure. When your work is to be judged, you will find that a balance sheet of how much you have received and how much you have disbursed as a representative of the association and how much net you have turned into the movement and how much morally you have helped the movement will be called for. If your balance sheet shows that for one month, three months, six months, or one year you have not added anything net to the association, your importance in it is nil, you will not account for much. Your status will be far below that of others who have been more valuable to the movement.

A president or representative who can show that for the year he or she has turned over $500, $1,000, or $10,000 net to the association occupies a position of eminence that calls for the greatest recognition of service rendered. Another president or representative may occupy no such position of recognition because of his failure.

Men and women are promoted on their record. Their record must be profitable. If their record is that of failure, they remain failures until they can prove otherwise. There is no other standard by which you can judge the ability of a man. Always seek to get substantial value for their work, because you will never be able to recall them as they move along.

Whenever you want to sell anything, unless you meet somebody who is badly in need of that thing, you are always going to be offered less than the value of the thing. So never buy anything for its full value otherwise you will have it at a loss. It is better to buy things for cash or on short term rather than on long term. A long term purchase carries a greater percentage of interest on the purchase. Something that you purchase on terms can be bought at almost half the price if bought for cash because people are also anxious to sell for cash even though they make a sacrifice of the thing, because they want the cash. When you buy on terms, you must bear the burden, not the seller. When you buy for cash, the seller bears a burden in the loss to get cash. Always have cash and bargains will always show up. If you have no cash, when you see bargains and want them, you pay twice the price for them, when you buy them on terms.

Never live above your income. Never live up to your income. Never assume responsibility when you are not prepared for it. It will burden you down. Never marry broke. Never marry before you are ready. Never allow anybody to force you to do anything against your will.

If you can see a thing and get good results from it at a cheaper price, don't pay a dearer price except you have money to throw away. Don't lose your head in thinking that something is going to run away, therefore, you must grab it now. Following that attitude, you may find your-self to be a big fool, because what you grab here, think-ing it is a wonder, you may find thrown away next door, not worth anything.

Always look around first, when you are in doubt. Try to find the duplicate. You may come back to the first, but if a thing is in the neighborhood with one person, it is almost likely that a similar thing is also in the same neighborhood. Search the neighborhood first, before you decide to lay all of your money on one thing.

Never think that one thing or that one person is the only peach in town. There may be better peaches on the tree. Try to curb your weakness for being a spendthrift. Every time you are tempted to spend ten cents or a dollar on a frivolous thing that you will not get any direct profit or return from, hold your hand, count ten before you do the thing, say to yourself "Have I any other pressing need or use for this money better than this frivolous thing?" There is always something else that you really need. Therefore, you will keep the money in your pocket.

Never give your money away outside of your race. If you are called upon to give it to God, ask yourself if God is really going to get it. Only when you feel that it is going into a channel that God will really appreciate him-self, should you give it, because God himself doesn't want money, but a good cause in his name may need it and you should first find out if there is really a cause. To send a man touring around the world in the name of God, for his own pleasure, is not giving to God. To give a man more worldly goods than he has already is not giving to God. To give to help carry on social service work in the community, or to help the poor of the community, or to rescue the children of the community is giving to God.

If you have to be critical in giving to God, be even more so when you give to man. It must be for a good cause and the nearest cause to you is the cause of your own race. Never fail to give charity where charity is needed within your own race, but don't allow yourself to be tricked.

If an old thing is good, don't buy a new one. Don't follow fashion for fashion's sake. Follow your own judgement for intelligence sake. If nothing is wrong with your suit of clothes, don't buy a new one because someone else has done so. All it may need is attention and so with everything. You may badly need the money later on, that you may spend on a new suit.

It is better to have the money than the thing, because when trouble comes you can run with your money, but you may not be able to carry all the things. The largest sum of money can be carried in your pocketbook; while the weight of other things may cause you to wait for the next train, and by waiting you may lose. Put your values more in money than in things. Only have those things that are necessary.

If you have the ambition to be greater than you are and you don't have the means to immediately do so, then practice rigid thrift in your present position by saving as much as you can so that in a given period of time, you will be able to change your position to reach your objective. Never consume all you have and then expect to climb higher, it cannot be done. Never go into anything in business that you know nothing about. No fool can make a success of anything. Therefore, know your business before you go into it, to make a profit out of it.

Never live on the capital of your business; you must live on the profit.

If you start to live on the capital, there will soon be no capital and no business. If you mean to stay in that business, whatever the profit is, live only on that profit, and not on all of that profit. Otherwise, the time may come when you have to live on the capital because you made no profit for that period. Business is only successful when you are making profit and not spending all the profit.

Whenever an enemy or any person attempts to create prejudice against your organization with the government, take immediate steps to counteract the statement and reassure the government that you have no intention of doing anything not in keeping with the law. Always watch for this because the government can easily outlaw your organization and curtail or prevent your activities. Therefore, don't join any movement that the government is not favorably inclined to tolerate; chiefly Communism.

Let the Communists fight their own battles. Let other people carry on their own discord. Have nothing to do with them. The more they carry on discord and you keep away from it, the better it will be for you because by keeping your head, you will be able to see more clearly and get an advantage.

Never let the government put you on the defensive. It will create prejudice against you.

Keep out of court as much as you can. If possible, never go there except to do social service work to help others. Try to never be charged with a crime, or be on trial. It will affect the association and affect you. Always try first to settle racial disputes without going to the law. Law is expensive and uncertain.

When you go to the law too often, you establish a bad record and when anybody wants to know anything about you, particularly government officials, they can search the court records. Keep away as a defendant. Encourage the people to keep away and not waste their money in litigation, if their litigation can be settled by you or any responsible representative of the race. The people pay too many fines in court. The money they pay for fines could be used for their families and their own benefit.

Always counsel Negroes not to be anxious to start litigations or to prosecute each other, if it can be avoided. Going to court too often gives the race a bad name and causes the government to think badly of the race. Always try to impress the government that you are law-abiding citizens, so that when you make a request of the government, it may respect the request.

Always keep your good work before the government and make the government aware of it, particularly social service work, charitable work, educational work. This does not mean racial education. Your racial education is private like the Jews. Make the government aware of all public education tending towards good citizenship. It should prominently be brought to the attention of the government.

Lesson 11

Man

Man, because of his sin which caused him to have fallen from his high estate of spiritual cleanliness to the level of a creature, who acts only for his own satisfaction by the gift of freewill, must be regarded as a dangerous creature of life. When he wants to he can be good, otherwise he is generally bad. In dealing with him you must calculate for his vices and his damnable evils. He is apt to disappoint you at any time, therefore you cannot wholly rely on him as an individual. Always try to touch him with the hope of bringing out that which is good, but be ever on your guard to experience the worst that is in him, because he is always in conflict with himself, as between good and evil.

When he can profit from evil he will do it and forget goodness. This has been his behavior ever since the first record of his existence and his first contact with his fellows.

Cain slew Abel for his success. Jacob robbed Esau of his birthright and down through the ages of human history, man has been robbing, exploiting and murdering man for gain.

Therefore, do not completely trust him, but watch him. When he is good try to keep him good, although he may not always remain good. If he is bad, avoid him. If you have no business with him, to the extent of being too much in his company, always try to reform him and use good influence on him because the hope of life is to produce a better man. The passion of man is in evidence everywhere. it revolts against affection, kindness and even love when it has a personal object to attain.

We have heard and read of children murdering their parents for gain and parents murdering their children in a similar manner. We have heard of wives killing their husbands and husbands killing their wives for gain. This reveals how wicked man can be. When we discuss man, we discuss the creature and not the particular individual whom we know, love and can trust. Man, therefore, is the abstract creature who is vile until we know him personally.

Seek first to know him before you completely trust him, because you are apt to be disappointed. A man shakes your hand today and tomorrow he is chief witness against you for execution. What is it that has caused him to do that? It is his vileness. Know it then that he is vile, and only when you know him sufficiently may you trust him as far as your judgment would dictate. He is apt to change on you and probably at the psychological moment when you need his help most.

Therefore, in dealing with man, trust your own character and your own judgment more than depending absolutely on his, for most of the time his advice to you is wrong and calculatingly so, so as to put you at a disadvantage.

Hear everything from man but do not believe everything until you have tested it for yourself.

The history of the world shows that man has been the chief murderer or killer. He has killed more creatures than any other being. He plans his murders which he may execute on individuals or on large groups of men and he generally does this for profit; national profit, racial profit, political profit or economic profit.

He is so vile that he no longer depends upon his physical strength to execute his vileness or to defend himself. He manufactures the most deadly weapons to do the deed quickly, while seeking self-protection from a similar attack.

Therefore, contemplate the state of his mind. Contemplate that he would calmly, coolly and collectively invent an instrument or chemical purposely designed to kill his fellows at a point where they may not harm him to gain the property and possession of his fellows. Can anything be more diabolical? No other animal sinks to this low murderous level. Hence man must be stripped of his veneer to see the evil machinations of his mind. The mind that makes TNT (high explosives), the mind that makes mustard gas, the mind that invents the Krupp Gun, the Winchester Rifle, the fast proof calibre pistol and poisons; all calculated to kill his brother. Do you want anything more wicked? Now, can you realize how bad man is? If you do, then always be on guard, because you know not when the evil genius cometh.

To be forewarned is to be forearmed. Therefore, know your man so that even though he comes with a smile, find out what is behind the smile. It is only a foolish man who accepts another at his word without finding out something about him.

Never fall in love at first sight and marry at the first opportunity. Never promise everything at the first request until you know the person is worthy of your promise.

If you prize your own good fortune never pledge it on the first approach of any man, but follow him, investigate him, and when his conduct coincides with what he states and what he promises you may take the chance of trusting him just so far. As proof of this, there are more unhappy marriages than happy ones, although based upon the best of promises at the start. There are more unhappy relations between man than happy relations, simply because the evil mind of man cannot keep good always. It is generally evil. This gives you sufficient evidence that man is vile and only in remote instances good. If you know it, then why take the chance of always believing before seeing? The taste of the pudding is the proof of it. Know your man before you believe. Never believe before you know. Always let your mission be to make man good, therefore talk to man always from the loftiest pinnacle. You may convert somebody; you may turn a vile man good, and if you succeed in doing this in even one instance, you have accomplished a great work.

Leadership in good character must make sacrifice to raise man from the lowest depths, but it is blind foolishness to sacrifice more than necessary; therefore, redeem the man with the least amount of harm to yourself.

Education

The present system of education is calculated to subjugate the majority and elevate the minority. The system was devised and has been promulgated by agents of the minority. This system was carefully thought out by those who desire to control others for their benefit and to the disadvantage of the others; to the extent that the others would not immediately rise into happiness and enjoyment of life simultaneously and equally with them. It was never originally intended to make all the people equal at the same time. Even more so, was it not intended to elevate the darker races to the immediate standard of the white races. The minority sprung from the white race to establish the system of education. Therefore, all textbooks and general literature are colored to suit the particular interest of those who established the system of education, and the group they represent as against the interest of others whom they did not want to immediately elevate to their standard.

There is always a limited process in the education of other races by the race that originates the system of education. As for instance, if a Negro attends a university with other students of the race that originated or projects the educational system, while the Negro would have the privilege of the classroom for general instructions to learn commonly, he may not have the privilege of his fellow students of the other race, who may be admitted to certain club fraternities within the university from which he would be debarred. Such fraternities generally enjoy the privilege of special instructions and special discussions which convey a wider range of enlightenment on the subjects taught than would be possible to the Negro, hence, when he graduates even from the same textbooks his technical knowledge is not as wide as that of others who have had fuller explanation in the technical interpretation of the particular textbooks and at the same time is only trained to reflect the system that props the intentions of the creators of the system, so that at his best, he who is making use of his education, is a slave to a system that was not intended for him, but to which he renders service.

Therefore, it is necessary for the Negro to be additionally educated or re-educated after he has imbibed the present system of education. The best way to do this is to educate him racially in the home, meeting hall or his own club, where he will be put under the closest scrutiny and analysis of what appears to be education, as coming from other people, because their system of education may not completely fit into the Negro's ideas of his own preservation.

By not being able to do this in the past, educated Negroes have not been able to assume proper leadership of their race, because their education was of the nature to cause them to support the present system which is of no advantage to the Negro, except as a servant, serf and slave, for which purpose really the system was devised, to a certain extent. This explains the behavior of leading Negro intellectuals who are not able to dissect the educational system of others and use only that portion that would be helpful to the Negro race, and add to it for a complete curriculum that would be satisfactory as a complete education for the race. Do not swallow wholly the educational system of any other group, except you have perfectly analyzed it and found it practical and useful to your group. There is still room for the Negro educational system, free from the prejudices that the present educational system upholds against him. Never fail to impress upon the Negro that he is never thoroughly educated until he has imbibed racial education.

It is by education that we become prepared for our duties and responsibilities in life. If one is badly educated he must naturally fail in the proper assumption and practice of his duties and responsibilities. The Negro fails in the proper assumption of his duties and responsibilities because he has been badly educated. He has universally failed to measure up to his duties and responsibilities as a man and as a race. His education has been subversive. He must now make his education practical and real, hence, he must re-arrange everything that affects him in his education to be of assistance to him in reaching out to his responsibilities and duties.

As you shouldn't expect another man to give you the clothing that you need to cover your own body, so you should not expect another race to give you the education to challenge their right to monopoly and mastery; to take for yourself that which they also want for themselves. If you are going to distrust the other man in his honesty because you know him to be dishonest, then you must maintain the attitude in every respect, for if he is dishonest in one he may be dishonest in all. If he will rob you of your wages, he will also rob you of your education that would enable you to know that he is robbing you of your wages. Trust only yourself and those you know, and those who look like you. Those who look like you and are related to you ought to be known first before you know others. There may be good grounds for a common education of all groups in a community such as civic education, political and social education, but this detail[ed] education that teaches man how to live to the highest and enjoy the best, is particular education and that particular education is always reserved for those who want to gain an advantage. Therefore, if in no other way in particular, secure education and have your own such as the Jews, who have outside of any common education, a particular and peculiar education of their own, which augments or adds to or modifies the common education that they have gathered in the community with others.

By view of the fact that the Jew gets a dual education, the education of the State and the education of his race, he is always in a unique position to worsen or to better his compatriots of another race in the community. He is always making more out of everything than the Gentile, because he knows all about the Gentile, while the Gentile knows nothing about him.

Lesson 12

The Purpose of Institutions

Organized society is always a mass of people, and as such, cannot do anything explicit or by detail by themselves. Hence, the organizing of institutions to do the particular work that cannot be done by the masses as a whole.

There are different kinds of institutions in a society, but each institution has its particular function, whether it be the church, college or university, school, hospital, academy, chamber of commerce, fraternity, trade union, literary club, sports club, athletic club, gymnasium, Y.M.C.A. or Y.W.C.A., etc.

In our present civilization, no society would be considered functioning properly if such institutions did not exist. Therefore, it is necessary for the Negro to pay close attention to developing the appreciation for institutional life.

It is not necessary or binding that he copies completely the systems, methods or manners of these institutions except in so far as they would go to help him to promote a higher life and in accomplishing the most out of this organized society. It is incumbent upon him that he also have and control his own institutions, based upon his own cultural and civilized idealism. As for instance, he may have his own church, but it is not necessary for him to adopt the peculiar articles of faith of the churches of alien races.

He is not a Hebrew, therefore, he would not adopt the Hebrew faith. He is not by origin a Roman Catholic nor an Anglican, because these faiths or religions were founded by white men with an idea of their own.

In his religious philosophy, the Negro may safely adopt articles of faith to link him to the Godhead of the Christian faith, and practice such as his particular religion, and so likewise with all other institutions.

His universities, colleges and schools may engage in the same process of education, but with an adopted curriculum necessary for the special benefit of the Negro. His clubs, academies and unions should be modelled in the same way with the absolute objective of attaining the end that is particularly desired by the race.

The Negro should never completely surrender himself to the institutional life of other people, otherwise, he will not be original, but purely and merely a copyist. If this could be appreciated it shows or reveals the wide fields which have remained untouched for Negro organization and Negro activity.

It is through the institutions of a race that the civilization and culture of the race are built. The Negro should occupy himself in cultivating his own culture and ultimately achieving his own civilized ends, so that in the comparison of racial achievements, he may be able to stand out distinctly on those achievements on his own account as others may do.

To live on the achievement of others is to really

admit the superiority of others, and the inferiority of self. As a fact, it is by such comparisons that the Negro is judged as an inferior being. Nothing that is handed to the Negro by somebody else should be sufficiently satisfactory to the Negro. He should seek to surround it with originality and then claim it as his own.

He is justified in remodeling and re-shaping the things to suit himself, because there is nothing new under the sun, whatever other people have. The Negro is the father of civilization. He constructed the first government in Africa and thereby taught others the way.

Always seek to improve on whatever you see fit to adopt. Never leave it at where you adopt it, because somebody else will claim it and prove their right to it. When you have added to it or taken away from it, you can prove that it is not the same thing, therefore it is yours. Always carefully and thoroughly investigate the accomplishments of other races. Try to improve and beat them at those achievements and keep your achievements a secret from them. Never open up the facts of your achievements to others because they are too anxious to get the last word on anything that is worthwhile.

Always hide the secrets of your achievements while demonstrating those achievements. It must be like a chemist selling his preparation or demonstrating it without giving away his formula, because the moment he does so, there will be many similar preparations on the market.

Each institution of a people has its special objects to attain, and may not fit in with the idealism of other peoples, so the Negro should have his own. He is not to be a slave to other people's idealism.

In some detail or other, each people's institutions must differ from yours according to their particular idealism. The Jew could never be a Negro in his institutional line, nor an Anglo-Saxon a Latin, nor a Latin a Teuton, nor neither a Negro. Therefore, a Negro must not try to be either, but in his institutional line be himself. Like the Jew, whom nature made a Jew for a particular purpose, therefore he must be different both in his habits, in his way of living and in his idealism. All people have separate and distinct functions and they should keep to those functions. The archangels in heaven have their functions, the cherubims have theirs, and the seraphims have theirs, and so with humanity. Following God and heaven's example, there is no reason why the Negro should not have his and when he doesn't he is not living the proper life in accordance with the purpose for which nature made him.

Your entire physiognomy is different from other peoples. Your hair is wooly, your nose is broad, your lips are thick, and so this difference must also be intended in your outlook and in your viewpoint on life. Anyone who tells you the contrary is a liar and a fraud, in fact, and enemy to you and to nature.

In this human world of confusion, never let anyone tell you that although of different races, you are one. If you were one, God would have made you so, because he is not a deceiver.

The Ethiopian is spoken of as being different. Even in the scripture it is said that he cannot change his skin. Think what that means. It is fair assumption that others may change their skins, but not the Ethiopian, who is the Negro, the Blackman. So there must be something permanent and lasting and eternal about the Blackman. God knows why he fixes it so. Don't try to change it by subterfuge or by inferential fraud. What a grand thing it is to know that while all other things change, you, because of your race, cannot change. Tell this to the world. Tell them how lasting you are and when they doubt it, send them to their Bibles, which you yourself never wrote. It emphasizes the greater truth that it may be so, because even those who wish otherwise have to acknowledge in this respect of virtue, the Blackman evidently was the first man. Adam and Eve were Black. Their two children, Cain and Abel, were Black. When Cain slew Abel and God appeared to ask him for his brother he was so shocked that he turned white, being the affliction of leprosy and as such, he became the progenitor of a new race born out of double sin.

The white man is Cain transformed, hence his career of murder, from Cain to Mussolini.

It is evident and fair assumption that when Cain ran away and disappeared from the neighborhood of his parents and journeyed afar, he built up a new race, living in the same country but far away, and in the process of time in Africa, where all this happened, the Negro race, through Adam and Eve continued their multiplication and as it spread itself in the development of a civilization, it came suddenly upon the settlement of Cain and knowing Cain's history of blood, ran the entire race from that neighborhood across the Mediterranean into Europe.

The white race of Cain hid in caves for centuries. Therefore, their white skin became fixed because most of the time they were hidden from the light. Hence, the white man as a European.

The World

The world is only part of the creation, an atom of universe. It is a complete entity of creation in relationship with other entities in the creation.

Man is made of mind and matter. Matter is manifested through nature, and mind is the connecting link with the spirit of God. The highest mind in the world is the mind of man in that behind it is the spirit of God giving the mind freewill to act through the soul. The soul is mind as well as the feeling of heart is soul and mind. The explanation of this is as intricate as that of the Trinity, God the Father, God the Son and God the Holy Ghost.

As God rules the universe and all matter and mind, so man through his mind rules the world over which he is Lord. The whole world then belongs to man. Each man should get his appropriate or proportionate share.

When in a lifetime he fails to get this, he naturally fails to lift himself up to his Lordship. One man's dispossession of his Lordship enthrones another man's sovereignty over him; hence, a ruling man and a serving man, a ruling race and a serving race.

Never be a race of servers, but a race of sovereigns. Lords, control the world, because the world is your province.

The world will not yield more than you want it to yield, but if you know the world, you can make the world yield much. Whatever you want, always try to master the world. To master the world, you must know the world, hence, you must pass outside of your own district, county and country. To know the world [go] and possess it because all that is in it is yours for the getting. Go out and get it.

There is no other rival but your fellowman. Never allow your fellowman to rise higher than you, otherwise, he will make you his slave.

If you do not use the world well by understanding it, it will destroy you through its matter and through its mind. If you treat the world well by knowing it thoroughly, the world will serve you obediently.

Always dispute the right of any other man's superiority over you in the world. Fear no other man but God, for God is your superior, but man is always your equal, so long as you rise to his attainments. You may rise to his attainments through the extraordinary use of your mind. *Mind is matter, mind is king, when it goes wrong, it loses its sceptre.* It remains right and wields the sceptre and sits upon a throne.

Always be on a throne, it is your prerogative, it is your right because you are the Lord and Master of the earth and all things therein.

In going through the world, hold your head and courage high for you must always remember that you are man and the ruler of the world. Remember that you rule the world through your mind. Think high, think deeply, think in a way to make you know all around and about you. If you do not know, you will fail. Be sure to know.

Knowledge is everywhere. It is hidden; search for it and when you discover it, and no one else knows about it, keep it and use it for the good of yourself and your race.

Your first duty in the world is to yourself, your family, your race and your racial nation. Then worship God absolutely and thank him for all.

If you allow another man to know more than you,

he will lead you up to the precipice and if it suits his purposes, he will let you fall in. Therefore, know as much as he does, and more, so that he may not lead you blindly. When you have to follow another man because you don't know, you are taking a dangerous risk. He may bury you. He may hide you away to suit his convenience. Therefore, while you walk through the world, always be on guard.

Try not to lose your mind. Try not to lose your mental balance. Try not to lose your sense of perception because in losing these things you are doomed in the world.

There is nothing man cannot know, except the Divine and almighty mysteries of God. All that is possible to man, man may know by seeking knowledge that is in the world.

Always try to be self-sufficient in yourself. Where it is impossible, seek that self-sufficiency in your racial relations, comradeship or in your race. Always see to it that your race is self-sufficient; that means that everything you want must be obtainable in your race as far as human relationships will permit.

If you are not individually self-sufficient or cooperative in your racial relations or self-sufficient in your race as a whole, you will have to go outside of yourself for that sufficiency, which will make you absolutely dependent on the goodwill of others for your sufficiency.

No one will give away value that is wanted for self, so you will have to serve and become servants or slaves to sufficiency.

Never wait on another man's pocketbook. Use your own, because he may never show up. He may die on the way and your wait will be too long.

Lesson 13

The Universe

No man yet knows the riddle of the Universe. It has been the eternal puzzle. Men in their searching desires are aiming at unravelling the mysteries behind it. It contains universal knowledge beyond the knowledge of our world.

If man can succeed in identifying the facts of the majority of units in the Universe, he approaches a greater degree of knowledge than those who confine themselves only to the investigation of things terrestrial.

The greater minds of our world have experimented and are experimenting in their desire to grapple with all the facts that sustain the Universe. No one knows if man will be permitted to enter into the mysterious realms of knowledge, but it is the duty of man to stretch his imagination afield, and gather for himself as much information as is naturally possible. Therefore, never rest with your limited knowledge of the world, but seek to find other knowledge with which you may be able to lift yourself far above that which has been attained or accomplished by man.

In the Universe there are mysteries which may be mathematically or scientifically measured and reduced to the concept of the human mind. Let your mind reach out then to the grappling of these mysteries by an approach based upon reason. As man before you discovered many things, gravitation, the fixed positions of the stars, the regular movements of planets, and such heretofore hidden facts, you may in the search, find out new truths upon which your race and civilization might climb to the highest pinnacle. Therefore, always carry an observant eye and an analytic mind. You may suddenly stumble upon some truth for which your world is waiting.

It doesn't matter who the person is, when he has discovered a truth, for which mankind is in need of or searching for, he becomes a hero and an immortal.

Try to grasp at immortality by leaving behind a never dying name because of the exceptional things you have been able to perceive and discover through the hidden mirror of universality. If you can see visions and dreams and make your visions and dreams true, you may focus the facts and the truths beyond your immediate reach by measuring them with your sublime knowledge.

Find the cause to justify the effect. The effect is visible everywhere, but the cause is generally hidden. Follow the line by degrees until you approach the start, the beginning, the source. Never stop half way but go right through, if you have good grounds to believe that there is something beyond. If there is a mountain, it is suggestive that there is a valley behind it. Don't rest with the mountain because you see it. Search for the valley because there may be much hidden there. Never cease studying the ideas or the facts that may lead you to a definite conclusion.

The things of this world have become common, because most of them have been revealed as far as we know, but there are uncommon things even on this earth, and much so in the Universe, that we may search after and make use of as we make use of things today brought to us through the probing genius of other men who saw the need for more and searched for it and brought it to mankind. Edison saw the need for more light and he brought more brilliant electricity; Stephenson saw the need for more speed and he brought the rapid moving engine with its steam. Fulton saw the need for more river transportation and quicker speed and he brought his steamboat; Harvey saw the need for conquering the mystery of the human system and revealed the circulatory system.

Observe well and see what mankind needs most in addition to what they have, and try to bring it to them. That is the way you stand out in immortality, as these men do stand out among us today, even though they are dead, and some of them have been dead for ages.

If I could lie down and dream out of my subconscious mind the dream of life, and find its source in a more direct way; how much more could I tell about life to astound and convince men of what life is.

It is the dreamer, the subconscious manipulator, who sees things by looking through the mental darkness. Therefore, see things for yourself, and see then in a way that mysterious Universe.

It is said that God is behind the Universe. No man has ever seen God. Suppose you, like Christ, could see God. What a wonder and an amazement! Christ saw God behind the Universe as Man. Christ was an object lesson to man's glorification and knowledge. Therefore, if you approach thought with its deepest sublimity, you may see as much as Christ saw when he saw God.

It is thought that created the Universe. It is thought that will master the Universe. Man must therefore use his thoughts to the limit to get the best results from the Universe. No thinking, no knowledge. Proper thinking may lead you suddenly into the conquest of that which heretofore was mysterious.

If man can think most excellently, then he climbs in that excellence to the companionship of the *most excellent.* As he climbs in his excellence to the most excellent, he shall not be presuming, but he shall be taking himself up to the most excellent; that which in other units was not excellent, and like the dutiful servant who used his talents and used them well, he shall be possessed of the talent of that servant who hid his and was ultimately deprived of it for the benefit of that servant who used his because he could appreciate the gift. Man in his excellence lifts himself highest to God by his mental industry, and the man who has no mental industry forfeits that mentality to the useful servant who climbs in his excellence to the *most excellent.*

Brush away the cobwebs of your mind, and see the Universe as looking through a crystal, because beyond you all is bright and beautiful. The darkness is in you. See the light! We want knowledge to lighten our darkness. Bring down the light and knowledge into your soul and flash it through your mind like the spark from the thunderbolt, and all creation will ignite in one glorious illumination, and you will pass through the mysteries of the Universe with the knowledge and eyes of a God.

If I could dream my life into eternity, and come back, with wisdom should not I have the surpassing knowledge of my fellows? Then why not seek it since it is there for man to seek out and to possess himself of it.

It is when you can reach up to it that you approach God's elevation. Not in rivalry of God, but as coming to God of whom you were always a part, but for the darkness of your own soul. Illumine the soul and God's brilliancy will be revealed as it was revealed to Christ, when the halo surrounded his head and He was declared the begotten Son of God in whom God was well pleased.

What a world of unfurlment. What a Universe of expectation to which man in his sublimity may climb. Why not be the first soul outside of Christ to climb in that sublimity to the *most excellent.*

The Greek Philosophers suggested to the Greek youth that he should know himself. Across the temple of Delphi was written these words. . . . "MAN KNOW THYSELF," but I may add also, "MAN KNOW THYSELF," and "MAN KNOW THE UNIVERSE," and "MAN KNOW YOUR GOD." In searching for this knowledge you may stumble upon the truth, a revelation that may lead you up to the heights of glory to be known as the greatest soul that fathoms the depths and reaches the heights.

Lesson 14

Self-Initiative

Every man is his own responsibility in life. Nature never made anyone dually, but singly, therefore you have your single responsibility.

The purpose of life is to live fully. Hence, the single life must be complete and in fact it is so with every man. Therefore, it is the duty of every man to fall back on himself for what he wants.

It is necessary for a man to use all of his faculties for his own protection. He always has a reserve of self-expression and action upon which to fall to protect and defend himself. Therefore, he must develop his faculties to do things thoroughly for himself. He must rely upon himself first for initiating all those things that may contribute to his personal well being.

Whatever he wants to do should first come from himself, as he should know what is best for himself. Advice may be helpful, but only to the extent that you have reason and judgment enough to see the value of the advice, otherwise it may be harmful. Very few people, if any, who advise others, do so completely honest[ly]. Generally, they advise with a motive for which the individual must pay the price, whatever that price may be.

Therefore, the best individual policy should be that the individual develop in himself or herself the courage to do things on his or her own account, always counting the cost in benefits or bad results.

The person who fails to be true to himself in taking the initiative to do things for himself will ultimately find out that he or she has been a "sucker" for others. Always surround yourself with the talent of being able to do by yourself, so as not to be too dependent. A person who has to depend on others, is not himself or herself, but the subject of others. A subject or a medium is apt to break under the influence of the controlling factor, as for instance a hypnotist who has a controlling factor, may so hypnotize his subject as to cause the subject to lose his or her mind. Therefore, try to never be the subject mentally of a factor; because a factor may destroy your opportunity for self-reliance and self-initiative.

Always maintain a strong will and emphasize that strong will even more when from the first reasonable judgments, you come to the conclusion that you are right. To come to that conclusion, you must have the facts before you in your mind. If your facts are as good as is known and can possibly be gathered on the particular thing, on which a decision is to be based; then don't allow anyone but God Almighty to alter your will, because *your will is your decision, and your decision is your intelligence, and your intelligence is your personality, and your personality is your self-confidence and your initiative.*

Always try to help yourself. Only when you are completely satisfied that you do not have the ability, knowledge, character and strength to do for yourself; should you call anyone to help you. When you ask others to help you over anything, be sure that they are your very, very, very good friends or relatives, because if the thing you ask them to help you out of, may be valuable to you and would be of value to others; they may take the value for themselves, and all that you will get for calling in someone else to do something for you that you should do for yourself, is disappointment. You will have the sad experience of learning how bad man is to rob his fellows of their rights. Anything on earth that is of value to you, is of interest to the other person. If you have a good idea, try to develop it yourself and master it yourself, before you ask for help; for at best, you will have to at least share the results with those who help you.

Fear God and Know No Other Fear

There is a God.

No man can say there is no God, because no man is like God. Man is limited in his intelligence at the most and man knows how insufficient he is between life and death; that he is born without his knowledge and dies without his will or wish; when his birth and death must logically and naturally be controlled by somebody else.

It could not be man, because man is always man whether he be a big man or a small man. So power that gives birth and causes death must be greater than man's power. Whatever that power is, it must be an absolute power.

Some men call it by different names but they all mean the same thing and it is *God*. Therefore, when man says there is no God, he is a fool for he is not as great as

God. Join no one in saying there is no God, and join no man in saying he is God, for it is blasphemy.

Fear God, but love God. If you love God, you need not fear God, for God is with you, and you are a part of him in your goodness. You fear God only when you are conscious of being evil or wicked.

You love God and work with God while you are good. There is nothing in this world that you should fear otherwise, for everything in the world is subject to you as man. Never fear man, but understand man, so as to escape the wrath of man and master man. Man is vicious, man is wicked, and you must know that he is. By knowing that he is wicked, you are able to handle him without fearing him.

Meet the stare of man with your stare. Never cringe before the stare of man, otherwise, he masters you.

Develop enough courage, character, boldness and self-confidence to look any man in the face and hold your ground. The first time you take your eyes off him because of his stare, he conquers you, because you are unprepared.

Look him straight in the eye; keep him covered with your eye, and let him bow and walk off, not you. This is the way man conquers the lion or a wild beast; by staring it in the eye; the moment he takes off his eye, the beast will spring upon him.

The daring look of man conquers man. The self-confidence of man conquers man. The strong character of man conquers man. The conqueror is the fellow with the boldest and longest stare. He hypnotizes his victim and walks over him like a worm.

Never be a worm. Try to never be obligated; for if you are obligated to a man, you cannot stare him to obedience; you will have to bow before him, because he has a grip on you. Try then to be free from all obligations to any man and thus always be yourself. God is pleased when man lifts himself to his true position in his kingdom of earth and heaven.

Look to God, ask him for strength, ask him for courage in righteousness, and you will be able to battle in the world of men. Don't ask him for wealth, but ask him for wisdom, as Solomon did, and he will open up to you the greater knowledge of goodness; if you are good in your approach to him through prayer for wisdom.

If you ask God for wisdom and understanding, you have everything else because with wisdom and understanding you will be able to take care of yourself. Therefore, never pray to God for particular things, for individual things. He has already given all that is necessary for your existence in creation and he has placed you as Lord and Master over them. Then, why worry him in further prayer for these things?

It is a waste of time, it is annoying, it is disgusting to God; if God can be disgusted. Seek ye first wisdom and understanding and all life will unfurl itself to you through God.

The mind and the soul are the receptacles of understanding and wisdom. Cleanse them with protection and approach the source who giveth them, and you shall be eternally blessed.

The Angels of Heaven are the good spirits from earth and the other planets who have passed through their probation of original life. No man on earth is an angel. The angels are spirits, not men.

Lesson 15

Personality

A thing to impress the world with is your own personality. Your make-up as a man or woman must be so clean cut as to leave nothing to suggest the incompleteness of a perfect person.

Man is always disposed to respect and honor those who show themselves observant of all the rules of manly dignity and character. It is said by some philosopher, that cleanliness is next to Godliness. Therefore, always be clean cut in your appearance; when you meet others and particularly the public. Never be slack in your appearance. At any time in meeting another person or persons, be neat and clean in appearance, even in your own household, because the moment you throw off the reserve of your personality you invite disrespect for your person.

As far as your personal attire is concerned, always see that it is in style, in proper shape and presentable before you appear outside of yourself. Always appear at your best, even though you may be suffering under the greatest difficulties of strain, because by that very good appearance you may win support to enable you to get out of your difficulties.

Never let your difficulties weigh you down to such an extent as to forget the presentableness of your personality. The world is always looking first for defects. Before they tabulate your virtues, see to it that nothing is defective about your appearance, from your shoes to your dollar, from your toes to your head, from your nails to your mouth; for in search of this, they will strike upon the one defect.

If there is one defect, they will say that you are careless about yourself and, therefore, will be careless about other things.

To maintain a good personality, you must observe all the rules of hygiene. Personal sanitation adds to confidence in you and complete satisfaction. Your appearance adds to your personal confidence. With this personal confidence you may face the world and win. With the personal defects, you naturally lose confidence and lose generally.

Never let anybody persuade you to go anyhow, even though you are not presentable, because you are not going very far. It may be just in that short distance that somebody of importance with deep scrutiny may observe you and conclude that you are a slack person and cause you to lose much.

A perfect personality, made through proper care of one's self is a passport to anywhere in the world, socially and otherwise.

Never go eating in the street. Never go into company and expose your bad manners in any direction. Try to suppress those bad manners; leave them at home. Eating and talking are bad manners in public, which are excusable and proper at the dining table.

No matter how hungry you are, don't take your meals while walking and never eat as an individual at a public meeting before the audience. You will lose their respect immediately, for not having regular meal hours and having your meals in an improper place which social regulations have established. A public platform is not a restaurant nor a dining room. Don't eat or even chew gum in people's faces. It is always an ugly sight and shows gross disrespect for company. You may chew your gum in your home, but not on a public platform nor at a public meeting.

The man with a good appearance walks down the street with pride, courage, self-confidence and self-respect. The man with a dirty shirt or dirty underwear and poorly kept clothes is self-consciously afraid of himself and is therefore afraid of company, hence, he is without confidence in himself.

A dirty person on the street is bound to be affected by the heat. The heat betrays his dirt to the passer-by and everybody looks around to see who it is, and as you are spotted, you become marked and the odor you throw off as a result of the heat may become your social undoing in the community. So always be clean in appearance and in body. It costs very little because even with one suit, you may keep it so clean as to always be presentable to the public.

It is better for the public to say, "that man has been wearing that suit for a year, but it has always been well kept," than for the public to say, "that man changes his clothes, but he is always dirty."

Never go on a platform with patched clothes because somebody will see the patch and surely come to the conclusion that you are patched up all around. When you go before the public, remember, that they are looking at you scrutinizingly, from head to foot, back and front. They are going right through you, searching for something that reveals your true character. Disappoint them always by giving them the best you have in character, which is outwardly represented by your clean-cut appearance.

I looked at a man. He was a beggar. His shoes were broken in many places and very dirty. His clothes were ragged and torn in many places. His collar was swarthy, black and revealed dirt everywhere. His fingernails were black and dirty. His teeth were unkempt. His breath was foul. His shirt was black with dirt. He asked me for help. I gave him a penny and walked away, because I thought it was enough, because he could not appreciate the use of more.

I saw another beggar whose clothes were poor, but clean. His pants revealed poverty, but they were also clean. I gave him a sovereign because I thought he could appreciate the use of it. There is a moral. People will judge you by your appearance, whether you are rich or poor; and they will deal with you accordingly.

Never make it a custom to carry distress on your face or in your eyes. Never carry yourself as to suggest despondency and over-burdening sorrow. People will learn to shun you. Keep smiling, keep being pleasant all the time even if you are dying. It is better to be a pleasant corpse than a hideous ugly-looking one. Show distress only when you may win help from those you approach, but be sure that you have struck a right estimate of your sympathizers. To show sorrow to those not interested, is to drive them away from you. Never show it to those who are not interested.

When you are keeping an appointment, always appear at your best to justify the particular mission. For instance, if you are going to do big business, appear in a way to suggest that you can maintain and live up to big business. If you are going to seek a job by an appointment, modify your dress so as not to outdress your prospective employer.

If you are going begging for yourself, don't go flashily dressed or overdressed, but dress in keeping with the kind of impression you would like to make upon your benefactor; this is purely a question of judgment.

If you are going begging for a cause like the U.N.I.A., you must not go as a revealed personal beggar, you would cause the person to say to himself, "why should I give him money for a cause when he looks like someone who begs for himself, and cannot be trusted with such philanthropic responsibility for others."

Never go asking help for a cause, caring not how lofty it is, looking hungry, distressed and broken-hearted yourself; nobody will believe your story. You are likely to be jailed until you can prove your sincerity.

Win a good reputation in your community by being up-to-date in your personality. Let your individuality stand out clearly. Every man has an individuality. He is known by that individuality. The background of that individuality should be his clean-cut personality.

Don't be lazy in whatever you have to do, because that laziness will grow on you, and people will observe you and mark you as being lazy. If the news circulates, it will undo you.

If you find a thing to do as a job or occupation, do it well and show interest in it until you have decided to do something else, but while you are doing it, do it to the best of your ability, and put your personality and individuality behind it, because somebody observing or coming after you will say, "this thing was well done by Jones, or badly done by Jones." Your reputation is at stake.

If you can choose your employment or occupation, then choose only that employment or occupation that would give you complete satisfaction in its practice, so that you may put your whole heart and soul in it, and achieve the greatest good or the greatest result.

To carelessly choose your occupation or employment, and find afterwards that it does not suit your nature, is a waste of time. If you dislike your employment or occupation, you will not concentrate on it and give the best results to your own benefit, because you will always be thinking of something else while mechanically doing what you are occupied with. Hence, to be your true self, always be sure to properly select the right occupation before you go into it.

Never be frivolous in the public eye or in the eye of company, because they will mark you down as a frivolous and irresponsible person. Always try to maintain the dignity of seriousness or at least a poise that would suggest that you are a person of dignified reserve. To go giggling, prancing and jumping about like a child stamps you as a clown. A man must be a man, a woman must be a woman, while a child must be a child. You are a child once, a man once and a corpse once. In the three stages you must behave according to nature. Prance and giggle as a child, be serious and dignified as a man and rest peacefully as a corpse.

If you happen to make a mistake in getting employment or a position that is not suited to your nature and disposition, while working at it, do the best you can to maintain your reputation, exercise your effort to find the occupation or employment you are best suited for, and see that you do not make a second mistake, but find your right place in life.

If you go on making mistakes of that kind, your life will end as a complete failure, because you will never be able to master anything, because your whole soul and heart was never in anything.

Before you can impress others and get them to follow you or imitate you or accept your suggestion of anything higher in life, you must show evidence of success in it. No man who is not successful can teach others how to succeed. It is impertinence for a man who has not succeeded through his personality to suggest to other people how they can succeed. Therefore, make yourself a success and other people will follow your advice, because they see success in you.

Never go among people better than yourself, telling them how to succeed, but use your illustrations of success among others who have not succeeded and that illustration must be in your own personality and individuality.

To maintain a good personality and robust individuality, be sure to keep your body in proper physical condition. There is no better way to do this than at least once a week to take some kind of effective purgative. It will clean your system and give you clear vision and healthy thought, with a responsive body, free of pain and ailments. Doing this regularly may lengthen your life from ten to twenty years, because it keeps you in a state of health to resist the germs of disease. If you follow this practice, you may never have to see a doctor, except on major physical matters.

Never try to make an important speech with a clogged system. The poison of your system will get upon your mind and keep you so hazy in thought as not to reveal the mentality of your true self. When a person claims to feel bad and goes to a doctor, except it is an ailment resulting from a major cause, he always prescribes a purgative. Why pay a dollar or two or ten to get the same thing you may take at a cost of five cents? A clear system is always a prevention against threatening diseases.

Keep your system clear at least once a week. If a motor car runs all the time without being cleaned or overhauled it will suddenly one day break down and it is iron. How much more will a human being not break down if he doesn't keep his system clear? Everything he eats does not pass out voluntarily. Some things remain in the system to breed germs of disease which may affect you in all ways. The greatest insurance is to keep your system regularly cleansed.

A heavy stomach or disordered stomach affects the whole nervous system. All the nerves are related in the human body and they depend on the stomach, chiefly, as a main artery of supply. If the stomach grows sick it sends poison throughout the whole body. Keep your stomach clear. It is better to be half hungry than wholly filled.

Lesson 16

Propaganda

Propaganda means to propagate or to make known extensively some particular phase of human intelligence. The desire is to convert or influence the people to the acceptance of the truth of that particular intelligence that is sought to be spread among them.

Propaganda can be true or false in its origin or intent; but it is always directed at the public for the purpose of winning the support of that public to the sentiment expressed in the propaganda. If you hate a man, giving him a bad name well may explain one of the purposes of propaganda without truth behind it.

Nearly all organized efforts have a system of propaganda to convert people to their principles and get them to support them even though there may be no merit behind it all.

Propaganda is all around you; to make you buy a special brand of cigarettes, although no good, but advertised to be the best; to make you drink or use a certain brand of tea; telling you of its wonderful qualities and its everlasting benefits when there is absolutely nothing to it, and so on.

Before the war of 1914-1918, the Germans were known to be the most cultured and scientific people in Europe. When the war started, the other nations in order to discredit the Germans and to hold them up to world ridicule and the contempt of civilization, released the propaganda that classified the Germans as Huns and barbarians. This also reveals how organized intention can be carried to the public for public acceptance without thought.

The press, cinema, pulpit, schoolroom are all propaganda agencies for one thing or the other. The pulpit carries religious propaganda, the schoolroom carries educational propaganda, the press carries out written propaganda, the platform carries on oral propaganda, the cinema carries out demonstrative propaganda. These methods have been devised by the white man to spread his ideas universally among men. That is why he is able, in a major sense, to control the minds of the people of the world.

The white man is a great propagandist. He fully and completely realizes the value of propaganda. Therefore, you must organize your propaganda to undo the propaganda of other people; if their propaganda affects your interest. The bible is religious propaganda, the school book is literary propaganda. The novels and books you read are also literary propaganda, all calculated to bring about certain results beneficial to the propagandist.

Never forget then that you are surrounded by a world of propaganda, all dressed up or cooped up to suit a doubtful public that is not careful about what it digests from without. The artist is also a propagandist. He paints pictures to convey the idea he wants to impress upon the non-thinking and doubtful public. The sculptor is also a propagandist. He chisels figures and portrays them to suit the aim or purpose he wants to achieve. The pictures of the Madonna and Christ and of the angels are painted portraying a white race, so as to inflict upon the rest of the world the belief that God, the angels and the Holy Family are all white, as well as Adam and Eve. Adam and Eve were black. They also paint the devil and the imps of hell black to impress upon the world the belief that all that is black is evil and all that is white is good and holy.

Tear from your walls, all pictures that glorify other races. Tear up and burn every bit of propaganda that does not carry your idea of things. Treat them as trash.

When you go to the cinema and you see the glorification of others in the pictures don't accept it; don't believe it to be true. Instead, visualize yourself achieving whatever is presented, and if possible, organize your propaganda to that effect. You should always match propaganda with propaganda.

Have your own newspapers, your own artists, your own sculptors, your own pulpits, your own platforms, print your own books and show your own motion pictures and sculpture your own subjects. Never accept as yours subjects of another race; but glorify all the good in yourselves.

Keep your home free and clear of alien objects of glorification of other races, otherwise your children will grow up to adore and glorify other people. Put in the place of others the heroes and noble characters of your own race.

Never allow your children to play with or to have white dolls. It will give them the idea of having white children themselves. Give them the dolls of their own race to play with and they will grow up with the idea of race love and race purity.

Watch the newspapers, magazines and journals daily for propaganda against your race or your institutions; particularly against the U.N.I.A. Rush into print immediately a defense of your race institutions and organizations from any attack. Never allow an insult propagated to go unanswered by you. Be ever vigilant to down anything by way of propaganda that dishonors or discredits you. Don't help the other fellow to carry on propaganda against yourself or your race. All propaganda comes from the arranged desire of individuals and not from a race as a whole. It is the thinkers and leaders who originate propaganda. By insisting on its wide distribution they get other people to think as they like.

Don't accept the thoughts of others through propaganda, unless it coincides with yours. Don't follow the band down the street because it plays sweet music to the propaganda of the circus manager. He may lead you into the circus tent and take away your pocketbook; that is to say, don't get on anybody's band wagon, because he may drive you to hell with his sweet music. Like the Pied Piper of Hamlin, who played his sweet pipe and led the rats out of the city and into the sea and drowned them.

Propaganda organized by somebody else is always calculated to take advantage of you. Don't help them do so. Always ask, what is this about? What is the object of this? Who has sent this out? What is he aiming at? Will it hurt me and my race? Is he trying to get an advantage over me? Is it honest? Is it true? If you ask these questions of all propaganda that comes up, before you swallow it, you will be able to take care of yourself.

Don't sing the songs and repeat the praises that glorify other races. Sing your own songs and recite your own praises that glorify your own race. For instance, it is foolish for Negroes to sing or say "Britons never shall be slaves"[2] when they themselves have been slaves and are likely to be slaves if they don't impress upon their minds that they as Negroes will never be slaves again.

Sing, therefore, "Negroes never shall be slaves." Be careful how you sing religious hymns that have been written, dished up and made popular by white writers to glorify the white race in the name of God; taking advantage of the silence of God to impress inferiority upon your race such as "the great white wings of angels," "the great white throne of God," "wash me white as snow." All these are damnably vicious forms of propaganda against the Black race. "Though my sins be as scarlet, they shall be whiter than snow." "Wash me in the blood and I shall be whiter than snow." All these things reflect the propaganda designed by the white man to glorify his skin and his race as against the black imps of hell and the black devil and the black pale of doom.

The idea of the white man making black a symbol of mourning and sadness is just to show the extreme of the purity of whiteness and it's joy and happiness. Reverse this. If possible teach the Negro that when he is in mourning he should wear white, and when he is happy to wear black. This is meeting propaganda with propaganda, the hatchet with the hatchet, the stick with the stick and the stone with the stone. Everything on earth is man's creation. So out of man's propaganda and mind he has created his special systems of opinion to meet his designs.

Therefore, customs are based upon acceptance of propaganda skillfully engineered. Have your own propaganda and hand it down through the ages. Write your own poetry and recite it. Compose your own songs and sing them. Write your own interpretation of the scriptures and history and teach them as far as the interpretation of others affect your race.

Challenge the thought of any book of other literature that dishonors or discredits you in any particular way; and give it the widest publicity so as to undo the harm intended. Remember always, that an error not corrected ultimately becomes a fact. Never allow false statements or allegations against your race to become current and pass into history as if they were facts.

War

War is the hellish passion of man let loose in opposition to man. It sums up the cruelty of man towards man. It always aims at the stronger taking advantage of the weaker to gain that which could not have been acquired otherwise; because of the failure to use human reason. War comes when men fail to adjust their differences with reasoning.

Always be prepared for the exhibition of the vilest passions of men in war. Man has always warred against his fellow man. It started with Cain against Abel and has continued down through the ages; and shall ever be so as long as man remains an unreasonable creature.

No generation has shown that man intends to become wholly reasonable. Therefore, in time of peace, prepare for war, so as not to be caught unprepared by your enemy who will naturally be the stronger, if he is prepared while you are not prepared in using the implements of warfare. War is not a good thing, but man is also not a good being. You must expect war from his disposition. All things are fair in war to win the advantage over your enemy.

When there is war, use all the implements at your disposal to defeat your enemy. Do not discuss terms while you are warring; discuss them after you are victorious. When war comes, all resources of intelligence and wealth, all utilities are placed at the service of those who conduct the war to make them victorious on behalf of those for whom they are warring. Therefore, have in view the obtaining and controlling of all such resources, factors and utilities that may be necessary as ammunitions of war.

There may be righteous wars as well as unrighteous wars; depending entirely upon the civilization that makes the war or defends itself in war. It may be war to put down human abuse in favor of human virtue. The warmakers have always justified war in some way or another. If you become engaged in a war, always have justification for your engagement.

If the war is not yours, get something out of it before you go into it and complete it for the good of others. Never go into war foolishly. Never sacrifice your life without good results for your cause. War is the best time to take advantage of your transgressor, whoever he may be. Whenever he is engaged in war and he promises you nothing, you will never get anything from him in time of peace. Therefore, during the time of war make your bargains before you help anybody else in war. If you are suffering from the abuses of others and there should be a threat of war against them from some other source, encourage it because it will be your chance to force a square deal. The more other people war among themselves, the stronger you become if you exercise good judgment.

Divide your enemies so as to gain your advantage. Always keep them divided so as to be able to gain the advantage. Your only hope of escaping the hate and prejudice of other people is to keep them severely occupied with other problems. If they have nothing else to attend to, they will concentrate on you and your problems will be aggravated.

While others have gone to war, try to be at peace among yourselves to gather the spoils of war. Never talk war openly to your enemies; but be prepared for war. If you talk it, they will become prepared waiting for you. Keep the other races divided and fighting each other as much as you can so as to take advantage for yourselves.

If they have no other problems to occupy their time, they will turn to you and turn on you. Keep them occupied otherwise. The more confused they are worrying over their troubles, the more time you will have to get out of your trouble.

Lesson 17

Communism

Communism is a white man's creation to solve his own political and economic problems. It suggests the enthronement of the white working class over the capitalistic class of the race. It was conceived by white men who were in sympathy with the economic struggles of their own white masses. It was never conceived and originally intended for the economic or political emancipation of the Blacks, but rather to raise the earning capacity of the lowest class of white workers.

It was founded principally on the theory of Karl Marx, who knew very little about Negroes, and who thought and wrote less about them. It is a dangerous theory of economic and political reformation because it seeks to put government in the hands of an ignorant white mass who have not been able to destroy their natural prejudices towards Negroes and other non-white people.

While it may be a good thing for them, it will be a bad thing for the Negroes who will fall under the government of the most ignorant, prejudiced class of the white race. The ignorant white man is cruel and prejudiced because of his very ignorance. Therefore, you may see how dangerous it would be to place in his hands, by the very strength of his numbers, a government dictated and controlled by him. While the capitalistic system is ruthless and bad, it nevertheless gives the Negro a chance for employment competitive with the working classes of white men; for the purpose of extracting profit from labor, irrespective of the color of labor.

The Negro not being an industrial employer shares, therefore, the opportunity to labor in competition with the white worker only because the white capitalist is willing to use anybody who can contribute the most profit to his industries; regardless of color.

The capitalistic white man is an enemy of Communism for the preservation of his own interest, if nothing more.

If the Negro is not his own industrial employer [and] loses the goodwill of white capitalist employers, because he is a communist, he will find himself unemployed. That is just what the communist wants, so as not to have a Black competitor. This will enable him to dictate his terms to the white employer and get him at the expense of the unemployed Negro, because he too is a communist.

The idea of the communist inviting Negroes to join their ranks is to support their theory that Negroes are communists too; so that if a white employer has to decide between a Black communist and a white communist, by the appeal of race, the white communist will get the consideration and the advantage.

Therefore, the scheme coming from the white communists is to make Negroes communists. It is a vile and wicked scheme. The communists have created their own party and organization of which they are the international leaders. They alone as executives, know the policy and designs of the Communist Party, which are kept from Negroes; for the purpose of fooling them into a sense of false security.

When it is considered that all the outrages in war, mob violence and extreme punishment have been administered to the Negro by the lowest class of white agents, as soldiers in war, as sailors, and as the mob, the Negro should have no doubt that his greatest enemy is the common white man who does not have enough intelligence to know the injury that he is doing to a race; even if he is paid to do so by his master.

All wars in Africa, in the colonies where the natives have been shot down and punished, were carried out by the common white man in the ranks. In the lynchings that have occurred in the southern section of the United States of America, the mob has always been made up of the lowest class of the white race. No governor, state official, or major aristocrat has ever been found in the mob or leading the mob. The mob has always been made up of the common, ignorant people, from whom communists are made up of and whom the party is intended to give political power and economic advantages.

The threat to run Negroes out of Jamestown, Pa. and the cotton fields of Mississippi and other sections of the United States were threats that came from the common white people. They served notices which stated, "Niggar, don't let the sun go down on you in this town."

It was the common white people of Cardiff, Wales, who in 1923 stopped the funeral procession of a dead Negro seaman, smashed the coffin, cut off his head and made a football of it in the street as a protest of Negroes being employed as seamen in Cardiff, while white men wanted work.[3]

In South Africa, East Africa and South West Africa, it is the poorer white colonists who practice the most wicked discrimination and persecute the natives to rob them of their rights. Everywhere it is the poor colonists and the poor white man who carries out the dirty work of prejudice against Negroes. These are the class of people for whom Communism is intended.

Consider that the Socialist, the Communist and the Trade Unionist of the white race are all agitating for higher wages and better living conditions. It is evident that these economic improvements must only come at the expense of greater exploitation of weaker people. The weaker peoples before were the Chinese, the East Indians and the Negroes. The Chinese have organized national resistance, the Indians have also organized national resistance. Therefore, only the Negro who is exposed to the most ruthless exploitation, is left to be exploited in the future. Surely the low class working white man will stop at nothing to raise his stature even as controller of government through Communism; even though it crushes the Negro. Hence, the Negro must realize that he is being played for a sucker.

What the Negro must do is to let the Communists fight their own battles and stand back to watch the fight. The Negro must take advantage of the opportunities presented during the fight, but he must not join the fight as a Communist, because he will be helping to bear the brunt of the battle with no guarantee that his condition will be better, but objectively worse, because he will help to transfer government from the more intelligent and cultured in behavior, to that of the ignorant, more prejudiced and most cruel.

The man who caught your forefathers in Africa was not the white capitalist, but the white sailor, who is a class of man from whom the Communists are made. He is dangerous to the Negro's liberty as a common man and as an ignorant man. Never join him to destroy the intelligence that rules the civilization that has given you existence up to the present time.

Any time you are asked to join the Communist Party by your communist associate or acquaintance, tell him in answer, "when you get to Russia, but not before then."

READ STATEMENT ON COMMUNISM
AND THE NEGRO IN
*THE PHILOSOPHY AND OPINIONS
OF MARCUS GARVEY.*[4]

Lesson 18

Commercial and Industrial Transactions

Commerce and industry are the feeding props of the economic life of the state, the community or society as a whole. On these two foundations rest the universal system of exchange with its financial factors.

Every progressive people and nation indulge in some form of commerce and industry, manufacturing or agricultural industry. It is by such activities that individuals find occupation within the normal life of the state.

You are either an employer or an employee, big or small. The employees are those who work for the employers. The employers are those who employ the employees and pay them salaries or wages. The employers pay themselves salaries out of their profits or dividends; so both employer and employee live off commerce and industry.

Those who do not work in this way are either wards of the state or recipients of charity or people who live off the earnings of others which flow from those who are industrious enough to work either as an employer or an employee. Every self-respecting man finds an occupation, either as an employee or as an employer; according to his choice, with his ability and general fitness, he earns a livelihood. All men try to earn as much as they possibly can. To do so, they generally equip themselves for their occupation. A good laborer or worker qualifies himself for his particular work so as to demand the best reward or wages. The businessman, proprietor or employer, generally goes into the most profitable business, so as to secure the largest amount of profit.

The man without a business of his own or without training to perform a particular type of job is always at a disadvantage in making a living. Great wealth is made out of commerce and industry, also the professions, which depend upon commerce and industry.

Commercial enterprises are of different kinds, as are industrial enterprises. In commerce, we have the grocery business, the lumber business, the ironmonger's business, the mercantile business or dry goods business, the clothing business, the tailoring business, retail and wholesale businesses of all kinds. Industrially, we have the manufacturing business that manufactures the particular articles of commerce, while the farming industry produces such commodities that are necessary for human consumption.

The industrious man must find an occupation in one or the other of these enterprises or professions if he is to be a proprietor or employer. He must have his own wholesale establishment or retail establishment. He must have his own factories or mills, either large or small. His capital may be a million dollars or ten dollars, according to the size of his enterprise. One proprietor has a chain of grocery stores, another has a push cart with his wares on it, but both' of them are proprietors. At the end of a week, one may make a profit of $10,000 on his investment, the other may make a profit of $10.00. This is due to the difference in the size of the business.

So a man who is enterprising with little capital can start a business of his own equally or simultaneously with the man who has large capital. One farmer may be the proprietor of 10,000 acres of land, another farmer may be the proprietor of one acre of land, but both of them are farmers and proprietors. Often it is the small proprietor who ultimately becomes a large proprietor through the success of his small venture. Most of the successful businessmen in the world started with a small amount of capital. Rockefeller started with a dollar and so did Carnegie. Henry Ford started with less than $50.00, but they both became great trust magnates in less than half a century. They opened the way for enterprising men who are willing to start with a modest or small beginning and work steadily to build a business of greater magnitude.

The examples of small men starting small businesses and building them up to massive concerns are common. In England, Joseph Lyons, a Jew, starting with less than $10 capital, built the great Joseph Lyons Company Tea Room and Restaurant syndicates that control the catering trade in all of Great Britain. This was also true of Thomas Lipton, who afterwards became Sir Thomas Lipton, the great tea magnate of England. This kind of enterprising success has its counterpart in nearly every country in the world, where small men have grown big by entering a business and sticking to a business until it becomes a colossal success.

Many an Italian millionaire started with a push cart selling oranges and bananas in the streets of New York and Chicago. Many Greeks also became millionaires by starting with a small lunch counter at some side street corner with capital of not more than $10.00. Many an Assyrian peddler started peddling with a box slung across his shoulder, containing assorted merchandise, not valued at more than $5.00, to become a millionaire or merchant prince and proprietor of a dry goods establishment later. Many an enterprising boy started out with 35¢ to buy newspapers and sell them, the morning and afternoon editions, and climbed up to be a great newspaper publisher or proprietor.

The fault with the Negro in business, commercial or industrial, has been his inability to appreciate starting at a given point and climbing steadily, while other races have been willing to start from the bottom and climb up. The Negroes have always desired to start from the top, therefore, he comes down. No success ever came from the top, it is always from the bottom up. The Negro must learn to climb from the bottom up. He will never be an industrial or commercial factor until he has learned the principles of commercial and industrial success. These principles are as much open to him as to anybody else.

Find a particular kind of business that you would like to engage yourself in, because you can make it profitable, and start it with whatever capital you have. You can start selling newspapers with a capital of 25¢, you can start selling oranges with a capital of $1.00. You can start selling stockings for ladies with a capital of $2.00, you can start selling ties for gentlemen with a capital of $2.00. Find out what your neighbors want most and are willing to buy. Start selling it to them, if not in a shop, by going door to door.

If your capital is larger, your opportunities become larger and easier. But no Negro need sit down at his doorstep and mourn his bad luck if he has 25¢ in his pocket to start a business. If you invest 25¢ wisely at 9 o'clock in the morning, by 6 o'clock in the evening you may have 50¢. If you eat 10¢ for that day and carry over 40¢ to the next day as capital, from 9 o'clock to 6 o'clock on the next day, you may have 75¢. Eat another 10¢ out of the 75¢, which will leave you with capital for the next day of 65¢. Your 65¢ capital may bring you 90¢. Eat 10¢ and carry over 80¢ for the following day, and at 6 o'clock on that day you may have $1.20. Eat 10¢ and carry over the $1.10 to the business of the next day and at 6 o'clock on that next day you may have $1.50 and so you follow this method for one year and at the end of that year your capital in business may be $25.00 and your income may be $5.00 on that day, out of which you provide your food and still have a large capital to face the next day. In five years your capital may be $1,000, in ten years your capital may be $10,000, in fifty years you may be a millionaire. That is how Rockefeller did it. That is how Carnegie did it, and they left their impression upon the world as self-made men.

If the Negro is going to look at Marshall Field or Sears and Roebuck in Chicago, John Wanamaker in Philadelphia or Gordon Selfridge in London, England and say I want to work like that, the dreamer will never start, because nothing starts that way. Wanamaker had to climb from the ground to the top of his skyscraper by perseverance and plodding and so did Selfridge and Marshall Field. They all started from the ground floor climbing up. The Negro must start from the ground floor of commerce and industry and climb up. When he can make¹ a good handkerchief, then later he will make a gross, and then a million gross with his factory going at top speed. When he can make a single tie successfully, then he will make his gross, then hundreds of gross, then thousands of gross [and] his factory will hum and buzz with activity.

Businesses are necessary, shops, stores, wholesale and retail, and factories. These are the places where the majority of the people are employed outside of the farm. The Negro to be employed and to be his own employer, must have his independent farms, stores, factories and mills. But he must start them as the white man did, growing from a single room of industry into the mighty factory on the hillside of the plain.

Without commerce and industry, a people perish economically. The Negro is perishing because he has no economic system, no commerce and industry.

There are tricks in every business. Never go into any business until you know all the tricks thereof, otherwise, you are bound to fail. If you like to indulge or engage yourself in a certain line of business, spend as much time as you possibly can investigating from your friends, acquaintances or whoever you can approach who is already in that business or knows about that business, so as to have all the information necessary about it before you start. It is the people who know of the tricks in trade that make the most profit out of the trade. If you are going to sell ripe bananas on a truck through the streets, find out how long a banana fully ripe will last in handling, so that you may gauge the time of sale of the bananas that they may not spoil on your hands; so with oranges, salt, fish, meat, ribbons, hats, shoes or anything that time and age will affect. If you don't know about the particulars of these things and invest in them, you will find yourself losing money instead of making it.

No one goes into business just for fun or pleasure, but for profit and results. Study all the possible means of making profit and getting good results out of the business in which you are to engage yourself.

A democracy is the safest kind of government for persons of individual initiative who desire to go into business to live under, because it gives every man a chance to do business more safely. As a fact, the capitalist of today was the laborer or worker of yesterday. Most of the capitalists of our present age were workers fifty, forty, thirty, twenty, ten or five years ago. Hence, the man who wants to go into business commercially, industrially or agriculturally, and win a fortune for himself, cannot and should not be a Communist, because Communism robs the individual of his personal initiative and ambition or the result thereof. Democracy, therefore, is the kind of government that offers to the individual the opportunity to rise from a laborer to the status of a capitalist or employer.

Property

In acquiring property for commercial, industrial or personal purposes or use, always see that you get value for your money. The property market is regulated by the Real Estate Brokers or Agents and the Mortgaging and Trust Companies who take mortgages on property. These people create the rise and fall in property values to suit their own conveniences and their own profits. When they can get the public to buy at high value, they induce the public to do so. When the public will not buy enough to insure their profit, they reduce the value of property and then encourage the buying of same. When the buying takes a gradual rise, they inflate the values again to make the public pay more for what they have started to buy again.

As far as Negroes are concerned, the custom of the Real Estate brokers and mortgaging companies has always been to sell them property at one-fourth, one-third and sometimes, one-half and other times one-hundred percent higher than the real value. When the Negro is ready to sell, he never gets half of what he paid for his property, except in exceptional cases. It is always suggested that his ownership and particularly his occupancy carries depreciation. Therefore, to be safe, when the Negro is purchasing property, he should first go to the official registry of property transfers in his community for a record of titles to find out the price paid for said property by the last purchaser so that he will know how much he is being charged in excess of the last sale price. He should also go to the government registry where the particular property is assessed for taxation to find out the real value from the government point of view for the property. Government assessed value on property is always about two-thirds of its ordinary market commercial value. Add one-third to the government assessment and you will find the real market value of the property. Never pay in excess of this value except you can afford to stand the loss to suit your own convenience, because when you want to sell your property that is the method others will adopt to find out its real value.

Always be careful and watch your mortgage or the person you have bought the property from to whom you owe balances after you have paid off the excess value of the property and started to pay on the real value. When the mortgagor or the seller of the property sells it to you in excess of its value, he is always friendly and tolerant while you are paying off the excess value, because he realizes he is the one who is benefitting all the time. But when you start to pay on the real value of the property to have equity in it that will make it marketable equity, he becomes nervous in the belief that you may pay off property and own it. The more you pay off on the real value of the property, the more nervous he becomes because he is always counting on your inability to pay for the property so as to foreclose on you to sell the property a second time, so as to make a double profit out of the excess value. That is to say, if he sells you the property originally at an excess value of $1,000, he will encourage you to pay off the $1,000 with tolerance because all that is gross profit. But he is always hoping to have the property to sell to another person at another excess value of $1,000. He can only have it when you have forfeited your regular payments on the real value to make it possible for him to foreclose. Therefore, he may trick you into being off guard to pay your first interest and sinking fund regularly, then in the first lapse of unpreparedness, he serves you by foreclosing and gets the property in his hands again for his second attempt. This is the method of all usurers who take mortgages and property and who deal with property as a business. If you will investigate, you will find that the majority of Negroes in every country have lost their property in this way.

Charitable Institutions

Charity suggests the sympathy and goodwill of the fortunate for the unfortunate. The poor we shall have with us always, and no one knows who shall be the poor, and so we become kindly in our behavior and disposition towards those who are unable to help themselves through misfortune or bad circumstances of any kind.

To properly dispense kindness to those in need; society decides on the establishment of institutions for charity. These may be hospitals, homes for the aged, homes for the blind, foundling institutions, asylums, etc. All well organized races have such institutions for their own and contribute to and support them.

The Negro must also be interested in the foundling and the keeping of such institutions for his own poor. In giving charity to a worthy cause, nothing is lost. In fact, it is like casting your bread upon the waters to come back to you after many days. You may help to do good to a member of your race without personally knowing the person and ten years hence some relative of that person may help some relative of yours without knowing them. It is the bread coming back upon the waters.

To give charity outside your race is probably sending it too far away. But to give it within your race is probably handing it to your own relative. In fact, charity begins at home, and your race is much nearer to you than a neighboring one. So always find time to bestow charity upon your race first. Every Negro helped from the ground to stand up, is another man set on the journey of Racial responsibility.

When possible, always seek to help your Negro brother. Never allow him to fall, because as low down as he goes, he may ultimately pull you down with him. As high up as you can send him, he might ultimately pull you up with him. Let us then push everyone of the race up and not down. To help a Negro boy or girl to become a useful man or woman, is probably to assist in giving to the world a great character who never would have found himself or herself but for the early help he received from you or your charitable institutions. Try to educate the boys and girls who have no parents. Try to assist those who have no one to depend on. Never let orphans go astray or fall into the hands of other races. They will only make servants of them. If you help them within the race, they may yet become the leaders of the Race in some particular line of success.

Before you give to others not of your race, think first how much your race needs it and place it there. Never be unkind to your race. Never allow the members of your race to die in poverty. It is your fault if they do. Always put yourself in the position of the unfortunate fellow and ask "how would I like to be in his stead." If your feelings and conscience rebel against his condition, then help him out of it. If you can, and as much as you do unto him, so may others do unto you in your time or hour of need.

Whenever you find your own Racial institutions worthy, support them. In any community in which you live, always seek to have your own charitable institutions. If the public funds are used for charity, then seek to get a portion for your group; separate and distinct from that of others. Because you may not desire charity for yourself, for the time being, why should you not support the appeal for charity for those of our race who may need it?

One may be prosperous today on his own initiative and account and by misadventure lose the natural ability of self-initiative to become dependent upon charity. You may lose your eyes, arms or legs. You may lose your health without contributing to it personally, but purely by accident. In that case you would become a recipient of charity without your expecting it or contributing to the cause. So charity should always be maintained for its own good; to benefit those who may be unfortunate enough to need it, and the next person to need it may be you. No one can tell. So never frown upon a worthy cause and never refuse to give and support if you can afford it.

Lesson 19

Winning Mankind by Kindness

A touch of kindness moves the heart of all men. To be kind is to be generous and to be pleasant; to be inviting in your manner. To be sympathetic and thoughtful of the other fellow's feelings may cost you nothing. You should be kind because sometimes you can extend it by a pleasant smile or a pleasant salutation or a good wish. To say, "I wish you well, I wish you everything that is prosperous, I hope you will succeed, I am sorry to hear of your bad fortune, I hope things will turn out successfully for you, I wish you a long life and the joy and happiness of it," is a good turn. All these convey to your friends, acquaintances, or even your enemies, a beauty of thought and soul that wins appreciation and often gratitude.

If your friend comes to you for help and you cannot give it to him, don't turn him away with cold words, but with the words of cheer and comfort. It may bring him joy in his disappointment, even though he does not get the thing he had hoped for.

You can never tell who is sincere or who is honest; therefore, you must always be on your guard not to lend your money. Don't give away your money foolishly, because you may never get it back.

If you are in doubt that you will get back a loan to a friend then try never to lend money to that friend, because he will become your enemy later. Offer him a drink of water, a piece of cake, or a delicious fruit, and then express your sorrow in the kindliest of words, or your inability to help him at that time, and see that when he leaves the gate, you smile with him and win his smile in return; which is an assurance of parting friendship, which probably would not be otherwise if you had bluntly refused his original request.

Win the world to you with a smile, with the hearty shake of the hand, with a glad welcome. It costs very little. It costs less than an ugly stare or the fixed hand of unwelcome.

In the organizational life of the U.N.I.A., always give to those you want to win. Give to the poor in the neighborhood and win them over to you. Give to them from the charitable funds of the organization. Give them necessities and niceties that they need and cannot buy. Be kind to the little children of the neighborhood. Give them candies from the charity fund. Give them pennies to buy candies and these little ones will carry the name of the U.N.I.A. through the neighborhood. Then visit the neighborhood from house to house. Leave a word of cheer everywhere you go and then persuade them to join the U.N.I.A. If they are in trouble, console them.

If the organization can help them with advice, give it to them. If you cannot, recommend them to some officer of the organization who has been well trained for such work. Have this officer go there and give the required advice; but let your good work be seen and known in the neighborhood and in the community, so that they will always come to you for organizational help. Remember that the organization is for the purpose of helping the needy, the distressed, and to assist all members of [the] Race who need help. It is by these methods that the Catholic church has won the hearts of the people; by the charity of its sisterhood and its priesthood helping the sick, the distressed, and restoring them to health.

When people have recovered from their bad conditions, their gratitude becomes the pillar on which the church rests. Let the gratitude of the Negro people in your community be the pillar on which the organization rests in your community.

There should always be a charitable fund in every division of the U.N.I.A. and a certain amount placed at the disposal of responsible representatives of the Association for the dispensing of charity to the neighborhood in which they live. As a representative of the Association, the charity should be disclosed in the name of the organization to maintain its reputation in the community.

Let the tender touch of kindness be everywhere; going from the U.N.I.A. to the people in the community. When men will remember you for nothing else, they will remember you for the kindly deed, the touch of sympathy that seldom comes from others, which is the duty of every representative of the U.N.I.A.

Lesson 20

Living for Something

Life is an important function. It was given for the purpose of expression. The flower expresses itself through the beauty of its bloom. The vine expresses itself through its rambling search in settling its own peculiar nature. The tree expresses itself in its smiling green leaves, shaking branches and sometimes hanging fruit. The lark expresses itself in its laughter and song. The river expresses itself in its gentle meandering unto the sea and man expresses himself according to the idealistic visions of his nature.

There is a scope for each life. Let yours find its scope and fully express itself.

Man should have a purpose and that purpose he should always keep in view, with the hope of achieving it in the fullest satisfaction to himself. Be not aimless, drifting and floating with the tide that doesn't go your way.

To find your purpose, you must search yourself and with the knowledge of what is good and what is bad, select your course, steering towards the particular object of your dream or desire. Never enter upon life's journey without a program. Simpleton as you may be, you can have a program. No ship ever reaches port without a positive destination beforehand, otherwise it will drift on the mighty ocean to be overtaken by the storm or the ill wind that blows. The sensible captain goes to sea with a chart to map out his course so as to reach his harbor of safety. Your program is your chart through life. Everything you do, do it by method. Nothing succeeds continuously or repeatedly by chance.

You may get success in a particular direction by accident, but it was chiefly because that accident was the correct method in achieving that particular thing, and you happened to have struck upon the right method by chance. But trying chances that way a second time may bring you failure, as it generally does. To follow the correct method will give you the same results all the time. Therefore, make your life a methodical one. Rise at a certain hour, work up to a certain hour, retire at a certain hour. Do everything on time so that your entire system becomes methodical.

If you have something to do, and it ought to be done, do it with proper method or system to get the best results. Study it first, then go after doing it. If a thing is worthwhile doing, it is worth while doing well.

How pitiful it is to see a man living without a program, not knowing how he is going to use his todays and tomorrows. If you follow him long enough you will find him going down the ditch of failure because he has been traveling without a program. Observe the other man who has his program, and see him go from one step to the next with success. If you have a program, you know what comes next. If you have none, you have to improvise one and then it is too late to do it properly, and so you fail.

If you want to be 5,000 miles away in December and it costs $500; to avoid being disappointed at the last moment, start in January to think about your trip and make arrangements for it, so that when the time comes you will be perfectly ready. Make this a practice in everything, don't wait until the time arrives. Think ahead!

Always try to look beyond the present by calling upon your past experience when you are looking at the future. Analyze it, arrange it to suit your needs, so that when things come upon you, you will be ready. Don't let things come upon you suddenly. The man who lives in the present, preparing for the future always enjoys a better future than the man who doesn't visualize it, but who goes right into it unprepared. Seeing the future and preparing for it is a worthy object.

Always try to look into the future. You make slight mistakes here and there, but if you gauge it properly, with the experience of the past and the conditions of the present, you may strike an even or accurate estimate of what it ought to be, so that when it comes, you will be able to welcome it with some kind of satisfaction.

To live for something doesn't only mean something for yourself, but something for your kith and kin and something for your race. If a father lives for something, he ought to be able to see his children through that something, so that what he does not accomplish for himself might be accomplished for his children. For instance, an industrious father lives with the hope of improving his social and economic condition. He would like to live in a beautiful mansion on the hill, from which he can see the country places around; the valleys, dales and the lofty mountains. But he is working in the valley, living in a small cottage. He is growing older without his dreams realized, but he looks to his son and says, "if I cannot enjoy this desire of mine, because I may be too old, when the time comes, I shall make it possible for my son or grandson to live on that hilltop. That is living in the future! That is living for something. When the old man dies, the son inherits and when the son dies, the grandson inherits. Inherits what? That which the grandfather lived for.

This should be the policy of every Negro; to live for something to hand down to a son, or a grandson so that they may have life a little easier than their fathers before them. This is the way successful and great families have come into the world and great races too.

No Negro should be objectless or purposeless in life. Always have a purpose. To waste time in non-essentials is to be purposeless. Playing bone dice is purposeless. There is nothing achieved in the time wasted in doing it. No great fortune is guaranteed. No great art is accomplished. No structure is built because it is a game of chance. Playing pool is waste, because like playing the dice, it is a game of chance. Sitting around and going from place to place without an occupation is waste. Valuable time is going and nothing is being registered by way of achievement. When one settles down upon a given and worthy idea or occupation, such as, an engineer, architect, builder, farmer, poet, or a teacher; he or she is working on something that may become tangible in results. It is from such tangible assets that we build fortunes. Find something tangible to do and use your time in doing it well. It is better that you be dead than having no purpose in life.

Ella Wheeler Wilcox says:

Have a purpose, and that purpose
    keep in view,
For drifting like a helmless vessel,
Thou can'st ne'er to self be true.

The ship without a helm must founder on the rock. Why
be such a ship? Why not sail through life like the barque
whose helm is perfect? Be a captain with chart in hand
seeing his port as he sails steadily on. See your port,
visualize it and as the time comes, anchor in it.

The Dignity and Pride of Race

God made man as a complete and finished being.
[There are no] flaws in him but his sin. The race of man,
therefore, must be perfect in its physical origin. Hence,
there is nothing to be ashamed of as far as species is concerned. The Blackman's origin is as true as the sun. He
need not therefore apologize for his existence. His place
in the world is fixed as a star and as such it is incumbent
upon him to maintain the dignity and pride of his own
manhood.

There is nothing unusual about the Negro other than
he is himself as man [sic]. He is beautiful in himself and
why not so? The Anglo-Saxon sees beauty through himself, the Teuton sees beauty through himself. The Mongol
sees beauty through himself and so naturally and logically the Negro ought to see beauty through himself.
When the Negro attempts to see beauty through the aqui-
line features of an Anglo-Saxon, then he images the

homeliness and ugliness of his own features because his features are different from those of the Anglo-Saxon.

Beauty must be reflected out of your own eyes. A Negro must be beautiful to a Negro, as an Anglo-Saxon is to an Anglo-Saxon. The highest standard of beauty therefore for a Negro, is the Negro. Never allow any race to say that your race is not beautiful. If there is ugliness in a race, it is in the other race, not in yours, because the other race looks different to you. To the Anglo-Saxon the Mongol is ugly; to the Mongol, the Anglo-Saxon is ugly. Compare the Anglo-Saxon and the Negro; it is the Anglo-Saxon who is ugly, not the Negro. The long sharp nose of the European cannot be considered beautiful against a strong healthy, air-free nasal passage of the Black man who is free from those nasal defects that make health difficult. The thin lips of the European could not be beautiful compared with the strong, healthy and developed lips of the African. These are the ways self-respecting people see themselves. The round healthy face of the African is much more beautiful than the straight, sickly looking face of the European. Then why surrender all that is good in you and discount it for that which doesn't reach a standard comparable to yours and others.

Always think yourself a perfect being, and be satisfied with yourself unless you are a jelly fish. Never allow anyone to convince you of your inferiority as a man. Rise in your dignity to justify all that is noble in your manhood as a race.

> May race is mine and I belong to it,
> It climbs with me and I shall climb
> with it,

My pride is mine and I shall surely
   honor it,
It is the height on which I daily sit.

The Social Confusion

Man at his best in his society is always quarreling.
He is never satisfied. Don't believe that you will find in
your lifetime the solution for all his problems and ills.
Attend only to those that concern you and your group. If
you can solve your own group's problems in your community, you have done well. Let others solve theirs. The time
you waste running around with others and helping them
in their problems, you are robbing your group of that
much time to help them solve their problems.

Whether a man is sober or drunk, he is a disagree-
able beast. You will find it so in every community. So
search for your man and tame the beast. He is never of
the same mood all the time. At one time you think you
can like him, at another time you think you could kill
him. Tame him towards the end of your own social satisfaction, for dabbling in the confusion of others will only
make you more confused and your divided energy will
only tend to defeat the special purpose which you should
have in solving the problems of your race.

Never forget that all other groups in the society of
your community are looking after their own individual
group interests; and your interests except from the community point of view, is never theirs. Therefore, their
interests should never be yours, as far as the particular
group interests are concerned. Don't be disappointed if
other people shock you by their behavior; because man is
made that way. He acts that way chiefly because he is

racially different. The whiteman may compliment you today and abuse you tomorrow, simply because of your race. Don't trust the whole community then, if it is made up of different groups, because it is apt to disappoint you by being selfish at any moment as far as the division of particular interests [is] concerned.

Always pick out your interest in the community and conserve it because others are doing the same. It is only when you tread on the heels of others by accident that you find out that there are differences between you and others. Your mistake doesn't prove a fact, the fact was there before your mistake. It is always a fact that each group has its own individual and collective racial problems.

The whiteman can never be a Negro, and the Negro can never be a whiteman; except after eternity, and you do not live that long. You may be the same in soul, but you cannot see a soul, so the similarity is beyond you. What you see is yourself, physically, and there is no doubt that there are physical differences between you and the other man. So, watch your step in the social confusion of life.

Always remember that another person is not you, for that other person knows too well that you are different from him. He is always on guard to divide the line of interests. This applies everywhere all around; in your home, office, workshop, in the street and in the community. Your wife will grab the article and say, "this is mine," and refuse to give it up, although you thought you were one and what was yours was hers and hers yours. She always has a time to claim her own either in peace or confusion. So always have your own in the social confusion of life, because even you and your partner may have to run in different directions to save your skins. If a person is gone with what is yours in another direction, you may lose your life following what you should have been carrying with you. Never forget this. It is of great importance to you for your own safety.

You should always have your own fare to pay the conductor. You may have to walk while the other person rides, because you can never tell where confusion will spring up. It may be in the street near the neighborhood. It may be 100 miles from town, and it will be a long walk if the car moves off because of the confusion between you and the driver.

Always expect confusion in the dividing line in the social contact of life.

Lesson 21

History of the U.N.I.A.

The Universal Negro Improvement Association and African Communities League was conceived as an organization for the purpose of raising the status of the Negro to national expression and general freedom, in the year 1913, during the visit of Marcus Garvey to Europe, after he had completed an adventurous visit to the Central American Republics.

The concept continued to impress itself upon him until the conceiver was compelled to make it practical during his stay in England during the same period. To make it practical he sailed from England, foregoing a course of law which he had undertaken for the purpose of a profession. In June of 1914, he sailed from England to Jamaica, B.W.I., his native home.

In July of 1914, he got together a group of men and women in the city of Kingston, and there he organized the association. Meetings in the name of the association, U.N.I.A. and A.C.L., were held regularly. Later, he held meetings of the organization at the Collegiate Hall, in the central part of the city of Kingston, Jamaica.

A group of officers was elected and the organization came into substantial existence. Many meetings were held in different parts of Jamaica in the name of the organization, and it continued to exist in the island as an organization until the year [1916],[5] when the founder sailed for America. On his arrival in America, he visited Tuskegee Institute on an outstanding invitation from the late Dr. Booker T. Washington. At the Institute, he met with the Principal, Dr. Robert R. Moton and Professor E. J. Scott, the Secretary-Treasurer. He discussed with them the purpose of the organization which was similar to the present aims and objects of the organization, which have been written into the U.N.I.A. Constitution.

Mr. Garvey received very little encouragement and left Tuskegee to continue a trip throughout the United States. On his return to New York, he visited Dr. W.E.B. DuBois, at the office of the National Association for the Advancement of Colored People. He discussed with him the aims and objects of the association and the possibility of organizing the movement in the United States. He was very much discouraged by Dr. DuBois. He undertook to organize on his own account in Harlem, by first speaking on the streets, principally Lenox Avenue, during week evenings and inviting his listeners to attend Sunday meetings at Lafayette Hall at 129th Street and 7th Avenue. The meetings at Lafayette Hall grew rapidly in membership, with occasional overflowing mass meetings held at the Palace Casino at 135th Street and 5th Avenue. After Lafayette Hall became too small to accommodate the growing membership meetings, the Palace Casino was secured for regular mass meetings and offices were established on the premises above what was then known as the Crescent Theatre at 135th Street.

From the Crescent Theatre Building to the Palace Casino, the movement grew with such rapidity that premises were secured at [138th] Street[6] between Lenox and 7th Avenue, to be known as Liberty Hall. All this progress took place within 18 months of the founding of the organization in Harlem, New York.

From Liberty Hall, the movement spread all over the United States and all over the world, culminating in the calling and convening of the first International Convention of the Negro Peoples of the World, in August 1920, in New York. At that convention, Marcus Garvey was elected President-General with 20 other persons making up the Executive Council to help guide the destiny of the organization that had become international.

For further information on the history of the U.N.I.A. and A.C.L., read the first and second volumes of *The Philosophy and Opinions of Marcus Garvey.*

How to Teach the U.N.I.A.

To know what the U.N.I.A. is, you must first read its constitution and books of laws, from cover to cover. You must also read the literature written by the founder bearing on the activities of the organization. The Preamble of the Constitution is vitally important to those who are to interpret its supreme object. Whenever the purpose of the organization is challenged by foes in particular, quote the Preamble of the Constitution. This should be done especially when the organization's enemies assail it before a court of law or before governmental authorities.

The preamble was written especially for the purpose of winning the sympathy and support of alien races where the other objects of the Association are being threatened by hostility.

The U.N.I.A. and A.C.L. was intended as one organization to carry out all the aims and objects of the constitution, but the laws of the states in which the organization operates separate the functions of friendly and fraternal organizations from those of business organizations. Hence, in the incorporation of the name of the Association in the State of New York in 1918, the two organizations were incorporated separately.

The organizations had to be incorporated as the Universal Negro Improvement Association Incorporated and The African Communities League Incorporated. The U.N.I.A. was incorporated as a fraternal organization and the African Communities League was incorporated as a business organization; but the Convention of 1920 accepted the original idea and linked the two organizations together as the U.N.I.A. and A.C.L. to hold the principles that were intended so that the two organizations would not go apart as if they were not related.

Whenever the U.N.I.A. does business, it will do so as The African Communities' League or as some other business organization; as evidenced in the incorporation of the Black Star Line, the Black Cross Navigation and Trading Company, The Negro Factories [Corporation,] etc., with all its capital held by the U.N.I.A.

No private individuals are intended to own the capital of any of these enterprises because these enterprises were organized as future ones will be organized, only for the purpose of supplying funds by way of profit to the U.N.I.A. to carry out its aims and objects as laid out in the Constitution of the U.N.I.A. in the interest of the race.

All subordinate companies of a business nature must be controlled by the U.N.I.A. to enable it to carry out the aims and objects of the U.N.I.A. and to comply with the law of the respective states.

Membership in the U.N.I.A. is divided into two kinds; the active member who joins a division or branch of the Association and pays the regular dues according to the constitution and by-laws of the organization. An active member has claim through his or her division to all benefits. All Negroes are considered ordinary members by virtue of their race. Charity may be dispensed to ordinary members if it is available and they can prove need.

The Association is supposed to maintain an interest in every Negro, irrespective of his nationality or his condition, as long as he has not been proved a traitor to the race and outlawed as such. *All the properties of the U.N.I.A. and associate business corporations, companies or enterprises are held in trust for the Negro race* in the relationship of the race through the active membership in the organization, as explained above.

The accumulated wealth and property of the organization must be handed down from generation to generation as the property of the Negro race, through the U.N.I.A., because it is held in trust to be given back to those who need it, as the occasion may demand.

Always give a receipt for money received in connection with the U.N.I.A. Always keep proper records and always have a duplicate for your protection. If you receive money from people in the name of the organization and do not give a receipt, you can bet they will investigate for the purpose of trapping you, and then your name will be dead if there is any delinquency.

When you attend a meeting of the U.N.I.A. as a

representative, and you are to receive money for the Parent Body, always let that money be received first on the records of the local division, through its officers, from whom you are raising it for the Parent Body for a particular purpose, so that when an account is to be made, the local records will support your report to the Parent Body.

Whenever you visit a division of the organization as an official representative of the Parent Body, you are then the Superior Officer. You shall then see that all things are conducted in the proper way in your presence in accordance with the constitution. When visiting a division, always make your visit profitable both to the division and to the Parent Body. Never create a loss or tax on the local division by your visit. Every visit you make to a division should be an opportunity for you to enroll new members for that division and to increase the enthusiasm of the local members for the organization.

In planning a visit to a division, whether it is a regular visit or otherwise, always inform the President and the Secretary respectively, and get them to make the necessary local announcements, so as to give you an extraordinary attendance of people and members, so that you may have an opportunity to increase the local membership.

If your visits are always an asset to the division, they will always invite you outside of your regular visitations to come among them. The expenses of your trip should be well figured out before you make it; railroad fare to and fro or bus fare to and fro, accommodations, etc. Hence, you should see that the meetings are worked up to such magnitude so that when they are held, they will cover these expenses.

When you visit a division in your territory, your financial returns should not be only from the division, but you should seek to use the time that you are in the community to get support from individuals and to do work for the Association, thereby killing two birds with the same stone.

You should always observe the proper form of opening and closing a meeting, as well as the proper form for conducting the meetings of the Association. They are as follows:

1. Opening hymn, "From Greenland's Icy Mountains."
2. Reading of the prayers in the ritual or hymn sheet of the Association. When your program is not too crowded and the time for meeting is lengthy, you may go through the whole form of prayers. If there is not sufficient time, read only such parts of the prayers as would enable you to go through the program without length.
3. After the prayers, sing either "Shine on Eternal Light," or "O Africa Awaken," then go into the rest of the program. When you are closing the program, close with the prayers of the Association for that purpose and sing the African National Anthem.

Whenever your object is to raise financial assistance or collection for the Parent Body or for the local division, let the raising of the same come in the middle of the program, after your most emphatic speech of the day is delivered, whether it is to be delivered by yourself or somebody else.

If you have things to dispose of for the Association or other help to get, this must come after the main collection. If you are the person appealing for the collection, you must do so with steady emphasis and a properly worded appeal. This must never be done half-heartedly because it will bring half-hearted results.

If you have raised a collection for the Parent Body at a meeting, see to it that it has been properly accounted for, after it is taken up. Make sure that it is not mixed up with the funds of the local division.

When visiting a division, you are always the guest of that division. The president presides and then introduces you. If it is a special business meeting where you have been called in to regulate the affairs of the division, you will take the chair as a representative of the Parent Body and conduct the meeting accordingly and restore order and then hand the meeting back to the president of the responsible officer of the division.

When a president has been removed and you have been called in, you may appoint someone temporarily, such as the vice-president, to act until you have reported the matter to the Parent Body, and the Parent Body carries out an appointment.

If there happen to be factions in a division and you are called in to straighten out their affairs, *never take up residence at the home of either side.* Seek independent lodging until you have disposed of the matter. Otherwise, you will have the prejudice against you for taking sides. *Never listen to one side without hearing the other side. Never give a decision on one side without hearing the other side.*

Always try to pacify, always try to bring factions together in keeping with the principles of the Association. Always try to compromise the factions towards keeping the peace. Whenever you make your official visit to the division as a representative of the Parent Body, always call for the records. Go through them and see that they are properly kept and then make a report to the Parent Body. Whenever you see mistakes that can be corrected, see that they are corrected. Don't allow them to continue.

Never allow any division to have individuals owning the property of the division in their names, except in cases where proper documents have been passed, where the organization is not registered, as between the persons and the organization, showing that they are only holding such in trust for the organization. But all this should be discouraged and immediate steps taken to register the organization in the particular state or community, so that its property may be held in its name.

When property is bought in the name of the organization, the organization's name must be mentioned and only the names of the officers of the organization at that time must appear as officers, not as individuals. For instance, Brooklyn Division of the U.N.I.A., John Brown, President, Henry Jones, Secretary. In law the names are taken as being officers of an organization. Hence, the individuals can make no separate claim on the property as individuals. Should they not continue as officers of the organization, those who then become officers of the organization would have their names substituted as officers.

This would not affect the ownership of the property by the organization.

Pay careful attention to this, so that the Association may not be defrauded of its property or its rights. Always look out for self-seeking officers and individuals in a division. See to it that they do nothing detrimental to the interests of the organization.

Always confine yourself to your own designated territory and never go beyond it, except when authorized to do so. Always respect the charter rights of every division, chapter, branch or affiliated organization. Never use one against the other as long as they are chartered. Have no favorite division, except the one that you may be a member of. Always hold an even balance. Always encourage co-operation between the divisions. If a member cannot get along in one division, before his membership is lost, advise him to join another division.

Wherever there are no divisions or chapters and there are Negroes in the community, encourage the organizing of a branch, chapter or a division. Over 1,000 Negroes in a community ought to have a division or a chapter, so in a community where you have 200,000 Negroes, you may have many divisions, according to the district and location. All 200,000 of those Negroes could belong to one or two divisions.

You should approach ministers of the gospel in the community and ask them to organize chapters in their churches of which they will be the presidents, so as to get their church members to be U.N.I.A. members. Do the same with lodges and fraternities. They can also be chapters of the U.N.I.A., even though they are independent lodges and fraternities.

Arguments for the Continuation, Perpetuation and Support of the U.N.I.A.

The U.N.I.A.'s Work from 1917-1937

1. The U.N.I.A. has stirred the entire world of Negroes to a consciousness of race pride which never existed before.

2. The U.N.I.A. broke down the barriers of racial nationality among Negroes and caused American, African, West Indian, Canadian, Australian and South and Central American Negroes to realize that they have a common interest.

3. The U.N.I.A. has given Negroes throughout the world a program of racial nationalism which never existed before.

4. The Association caused all Negroes to recognize their common origin as Africans and their African descent.

5. It has caused all the other races to recognize the national aspirations of the Negro. It placed the Negro's cause before the League of Nations and the Versailles Peace Conference.

6. It placed the national aspirations of the Negro before the Disarmament Conference in Washington, in 1924.

7. The U.N.I.A. caused the French, English and other European governments with colonies in Africa and the West Indies to extend greater privileges to the

native race and to offer them more secure positions in the respective civil service, diplomatic service and political life of the country.

8. Negro justices, magistrates and heads of government departments were appointed because of the activities of the U.N.I.A. in different countries.

9. The economic status of Negroes was raised in different countries because of the Association.

10. The Association taught the Negro how to go into big business.

11. It taught the Negro how to secure his own business enterprises through which tens of thousands of Negro businesses have been started all over the world.

12. It taught Negroes how to support their own professional men; doctors, lawyers, etc.

13. The U.N.I.A. taught the Negro how to support his own church.

14. It taught the Negro how to use his political power from which he has benefitted in the United States, the West Indies, Africa and other countries.

15. The U.N.I.A. gave the Negro a national flag and a national hymn.

16. It caused the other races to spell the word "Negro" with a capital "N."

17. It taught Negroes self-respect for their race.

18. It brought courage to the Negro race throughout the world.

19. It caused the Negro to search for a new type of leadership.

20. It taught the Negro preparedness against adversity.

21. It has been the most outstanding Negro organization throughout the world.

22. It is the most recognized international organization among Negroes.

23. It is known in all parts of the world.

24. It has taught the Negro to follow only Negro leadership.

25. It has saved the Negro from the hypocritical, dishonest leadership of other people which has never brought the Negro any good results.

26. It taught the Negro that the cats don't lead the rats, nor the lions the sheep, nor the wolves the foxes, and so Negroes should lead Negroes.

27. The U.N.I.A. has taught the Negro to never rely upon the sweet sounding words and promises of others, but to rely on his words and his own promises if he is to be led safely.

28. It has taught the Negro to believe in himself and not to believe that what another man seeks for himself he is going to give away freely.

29. It has taught the Negro to have his own labor organizations and not to expect other laborers who are competing with him for the same employment, to give honest leadership for him to compete with them for the same job.

30. It is the only organization that has given the Negro an international outlook.

31. It gave the Negro press a broader point of view.

32. It has kept the Negro from going RED for the convenience of others.

33. In twenty years the U.N.I.A. changed the attitude of the Negro and set him on the way to a new hope.

34. One of the fundamental desires of the U.N.I.A. is to approach every Negro with the attitude of friendship, brotherhood and sympathy. Therefore, every representative of the association must adopt an attitude that works to bring about the realization of such a desire.

It may be necessary to use a great amount of tolerance to reach the desired end, but whatever is necessary must be done to bring about such a state of affairs. The policy is that you cannot drive a Negro away from the organization and still want to organize all the Negroes. Every Negro that is lost prevents the ultimate achievement of the aims of the organization; so never try to drive a member out of the organization. Hold him and convert him.

Always appreciate the fact that the majority of Negroes are ignorant, and you must exercise a great amount of tolerance to educate them to your point of view. This is your missionary work. As other people were willing to sacrifice their time and even their lives to christianize our race, so we must exercise patience and time to civilize our people.

The attitude of expelling members and suspending members is not accepted with good grace, and should be resorted to only under the most extreme circumstances. The attitude should be adopted to find an alternative to expulsion.

The best way to prevent dissatisfaction in a division is to live up to the constitution and by-laws because it is only with the constitution and by-laws that you can discipline a member. If a member violates the constitution and by-laws, you can reasonably draw the violation to his or her attention.

You cannot show partiality in a division of the Association or in the work of the Association. You must be impartial to maintain the principles of the Association as the attraction for those who do not know anything about the Association.

Never cease in your efforts to influence a Negro to join the Association until he has joined. So long as he stays out of the U.N.I.A., the work of uniting all the Negroes cannot be accomplished. Always remember that you are a missionary for the cause of the Association, so lose no opportunity that may present itself to make converts for the Association.

A splendid way of proselyting for the Association is to interest all your friends and acquaintances in its movements. Whenever you go among them, tell them of anything done and accomplished by the Association.

Always find some work for the Association. During the time you are not actually attending a meeting of the Association or doing any special work for the Association, devote your time in calling upon your acquaintances in the neighborhood in your community to talk them into becoming members and supporters of the Association.

You should know all the people of your race on your street, in your neighborhood and in your town. Approach them in your leisure hours, one by one, to convert them to the organization and to get support from them for the organization.

Where you come across responsible people of the race, take their names, professions and addresses after talking to them about the Association, and send the same in a weekly report or a monthly report to the President-General's office at headquarters. Ask the President-General to communicate with these persons in the manner you think would best help to clinch the support of these persons for the organization. In your own town, secure the names, addresses and professions of all the responsible people, doctors, lawyers, merchants, preachers, etc. Send these names to headquarters with comments about each person for headquarters to help influence these persons to support the organization.

Always keep in touch with the newspapers published in your community. Get the newspaper publishers to print favorable news about the activities of the organization.

See to it that every intelligent person in the community, of the race, subscribes to or purchases the *Black Man,* so that they may keep up with the activities of the movement. Read the *Black Man* regularly yourself, so that others will not have information you have not got.

When you attend meetings of divisions as an official, always carry yourself with dignity and always be impartial in dealing with the affairs of the divisions. If you take sides not based on the constitution, you are only destroying your own usefulness in that division and to the Parent Body.

Your honor must always be uppermost in dealing with matters affecting the divisions when you visit them. If you are an official of the Parent Body, always see that the dignity of the Parent Body is maintained through you. Any bad behavior on your part, will reflect upon the judgment of the Parent Body in appointing you.

If you are a representative of the Parent Body with proper credentials, you must observe the agreement entered into between you and the Parent Body for dealing with the affairs of the Association. Any violation of the agreement may cause you to lose your office as a representative of the Parent Body.

Never overstep your authority in dealing with a division as a representative of the Parent Body. Never attempt to show your grand superiority to the displeasure of members of the division or officers of the division. Be as modest, yet as firm as you can be in your dealings. Nothing invites antagonism more than an arrogant and unreasonable display of power. The most powerful people in the world are the most modest when dealing with those whose goodwill they depend on. They know how much immodesty offends others. Never try to be offensive. Never threaten others, but reason with them. To threaten an officer or a member is to invite antagonism and belligerence, which will make your task more difficult.

Never enter into any unworthy arrangement with officers or members of divisions, because ultimately they will expose you when you do not do things to suit them. The moment you enter into any dishonorable arrangement, the person you have done so with, holds it as a club over your head and will place you in a false position. In order not to expose yourself, don't do it.

When working as a representative in a community, to get results for the association, you should divide that community into zones or districts. You may even reduce the districts to streets or blocks of streets and appoint some responsible and enthusiastic member in that zone, district or street to be a kind of captain or lieutenant to keep the spirit of the people in the area regulated to the principles of the organization. The captain or lieutenant must be an active member of the division. Since he lives on the street, he would likely know all the people on the street and could help greatly in organizing them as members of the organization.

Your chief aim must be to organize every man, woman and child. If with all this material and possibilities, you cannot make the U.N.I.A. succeed in that community, you yourself are a colossal failure and not the people. The greatest recognition of your merit and ability will be reflected by the number of people who are members of the Association in your community, district, town or state. Their activities will testify to your greater activity in their midst.

You should not expect promotion from the Parent Body except you have something to recommend you in your community for such promotion; otherwise your promotion will not be fair to someone else who has done his or her work. Don't complain, do the job! Get results! The moment you start to complain, you are stating that the thing cannot be done. If you cannot do it at one place, you cannot do it at another. You are a failure, you are no good.

Let your pride be in winning over an adversary. It gives good satisfaction. You have enough material in the U.N.I.A. to use as an argument against any man who is a member of the race, caring not how destructive he is. Therefore, don't leave him until you have converted him; talk him out. In this respect, bring all of your diplomacy to bear. Use all the experience you have had in dealing with men and enlarge on and explain every good point of the U.N.I.A. Carry your constitution and read the preamble and the aims and objects to him. Explain them as you have been taught them and when he makes up his mind to join, get him right there.

If you have approached him to become a member, let him join then. If you have approached him for support, get him to write or give his support right there. Afterwards, immediately thank him by correspondence for joining or supporting, to give him an impression of your business-like ability.

The best time to call on people is immediately after meals, not before, because when people are hungry, they are not in a good mood. Call immediately after the breakfast hour, the dinner hour and the supper hour. If you are calling at the office, never call an hour before lunch or an hour before dinner. Always go smiling and pleasant. Don't carry a long face.

If you have been abruptly received and abruptly talked to, reply with pleasant remarks and smile your subject into changing his or her mood. Even a savage will admit defeat when met by a smile. If a person has a frown on his face, say, "I hope you are well Mr. Jones." That will put him off guard immediately. If he states that he is not well, sympathize with him and tell him about some remedy you know. This is good psychology to win your subject; or you may say, "you have a very pretty picture here, Mr. Jones," or some other thing, though not pretty to flatter his vanity, but to take him out of his sullen mood. If he is a smoker, offer him a cigarette. Tell him something that you think he ought to be interested in. You may hit upon something by looking at the things around him. "Have you seen the latest picture?" "Have you heard the latest news?" Then go into your subject, after you have changed his attitude. Don't start talking to a sullen man on the subject you are approaching him on until you have won him over to a pleasant mood. It would be better to go back and visit him a second time.

Always point out to him that the U.N.I.A. acts as trustee for the race. Help him to understand that every Negro benefits from the success of the organization. In arguing for support of the U.N.I.A., draw extensively upon your imagination and find an argument to support you. You have the argument of the success of a nation, the success of other race groups and always use the Jew as argument.

Among the first persons to be approached for help for the U.N.I.A. are professional and business men and women of the race. A better organized race will mean better business for them. Tell them that that is the work of the U.N.I.A., therefore, they should support it. Let them realize the power you have in your hand to direct patronage one way or the other as an organization.

To win over your new prospect, tell him that Mr. So and So has done so and so for the organization, but *it must be a fact, not a lie.* Then he will not want to be left out and will support you.

This must not be done for personal profit, because if you are found using this method for personal gain, you will be struck off the roll of students and be disqualified as a representative, because the moment the person finds out that you have used the approach for personal purposes, you have damaged the Association and your own reputation. Hence, you are of no use, either to the Association or to anybody else.

The first international convention of the U.N.I.A., held in New York, from the 1st to the 31st of August, 1920 formulated and adopted the Declaration of Rights of the Negro Peoples of the World, to which the organization is committed until the objects of the said Declaration are fully realized. The Declaration must be studied by each leader of the race. It is to be found on page 135 in the second volume of the *Philosophy and Opinions of Marcus Garvey*. In seeking financial aid for the U.N.I.A., always do so with confidence. The high and lofty aims of the Association and the universal objects to be achieved, can only be done through the support of each and every member of the race. This calls for the support of every man.

To gain such support, always impress upon the Negro that heretofore, he has supported white organizations, such as the churches, and he has contributed to their institutions without getting any direct benefit. He has even supported the Salvation Army. Therefore, there is no reason why he should not support a movement of his own that calculates to bestow upon him and his generations untold benefits.

Contributions to the U.N.I.A. should be generally accepted from Negroes, but where other people of other races can be approached and are willing to give help, such help may be accepted, but without any strings attached or promises made that would in any way compromise the clear cut intelligence of the policy of the U.N.I.A. *Such contributions do not entitle the donors to any privileges of membership or to any right to attend the meetings of the U.N.I.A., except public meetings as guest.* Their contributions should never entitle them to attend or take part in any of the business meetings of the organization. Their donations may be accepted in the same way as Negroes give to white organizations; without having any claim on those organizations.

Whenever donations are accepted from other races, the names of such persons when registered on the same account of donations as that of Negroes, must be marked with a cross, and when such donations are being forwarded to the Parent Body, an explanation must be given stating that such a person is a member of the white race or whatever race the person may be, so that no communication of a private nature will be sent to that person which reveals the business of the U.N.I.A. This is very important, because by not distinguishing between the donors such persons may be written to as if they are members of the U.N.I.A. They may be sent communications that they have no right to receive.

In approaching people of other races for help, your argument must be different from that of an approach to members of your race. Your appeal should be based on humanity, good citizenship or helping a worthy cause. Never explain the objects that are of uppermost importance to the U.N.I.A., because they will naturally react with unfriendliness and suspicion. Never believe that another race is so friendly as to know your objects and not try to hinder you in ultimately succeeding.

Whenever you make an appeal to an individual or individuals for financial help for the organization, and you have failed in getting a response, the failure is not due to the person or persons you have addressed yourself to, but may be due to your inability to properly interpret to them the objects and aims of the U.N.I.A. and the reasons why they should support the Association. Always be in a position to interpret those aims and objects to gain support, because people are always willing to respond to a thing that is to benefit them, even in a remote way.

Never approach anyone for help for the Association with doubt in your mind. It is better that you wait until you are in the frame of mind to talk conscientiously so as to carry conviction rather than try to do so when your spirit is low. Let every day, every hour and every minute count in your life for something done, something accomplished.

Don't waste time, it is a sin. Time wasted can never be recalled or regained. Try to always be the best advocate of the cause of the U.N.I.A. Try to let no one surpass you in doing that. There is something in you that is individual, that nobody else has. Try to bring it out and let that be your individuality and personality; for which people will remember you and talk about you. There is nothing that someone else has done in the triumph of a cause that you cannot do if you go about it in the right way.

Always try to find the right way. Never hang around people who are always discouraged, despondent, poverty-stricken, poor and never-do-well. You will ultimately become like them. Try to get around cheery people, happy people, prosperous people, and you will unconsciously take on their prosperity and their happiness.

Never live in a house with or keep company with people who always have bad luck stories. Their sins will come upon you, for the same evil spirit that is following them may also be near you. Always appear bright when you are seeking help for the U.N.I.A.

Dealing With Divisions

In dealing with a division of the U.N.I.A. always recognize the division itself as a chartered body, as the representative body. The units of a division, according to the constitution, are all subordinate to the division. The divisional officers are the only responsible officers in a division. *No auxiliary has the status of the division.*

In dealing with a division, first recognize the officers of the division, according to the constitution. *The Legions, the Black Cross Nurses, the Motor Corps and all other auxiliaries must be obedient to the officers of the division.*

Great care must be taken in watching and controlling the activities of the Legions, because in ignorance they are apt to get the division or organization in trouble by trying to exercise authority while they are only members of an organization registered by the state.

The Legions' function is more physical, cultural and disciplinary than anything else. Any hostile demonstration by them that endangers the community or the peace thereof or creates trouble among the members, must be quickly put down and if necessary, their unit suspended to prevent such trouble. The Legions have no control over the Black Cross Nurses. The Black Cross Nurses are a separate unit. The only relationship may be that someone from the Legions, with the ability to train, may give them physical exercise and proper discipline. *The Black Cross Nurses fall entirely under the supervision of their own head nurse, who is to seek for them first aid training from some medical institution or individual, through the officers of the division.*

The Motor Corps is also an independent body of women who may be trained by a competent Legion officer, but with no direct affiliation. *See to it that divisional officers do not allow members of the Legions to appoint themselves to any office as lieutenants, captains, majors, colonels or what not without the authority of the president, who is the ranking officer of the Legions in his division, as set down in the constitution. See to it that divisions do not allow Tom, Dick and Harry to go into the division to speak to and lecture to them without the authority of the Parent Body, and that they do not allow anybody to use the meetings of the U.N.I.A. to put over their own propaganda which tends to distract members from the U.N.I.A.*

See to it that no fake lecturer or wild cat scheme representative gets into any meeting of the U.N.I.A. through any individual influence.

Keep a close eye on African princes, chiefs, princesses, and all such fake personalities, who come into the meetings of the U.N.I.A. No prince, chief or princess adopts such methods of going around begging and exploiting. Princes and princesses are royal personalities who stay at home or only make state visits to other countries and are generally accommodated by the head of a nation. Any time such fake princes or chiefs come among you, expose them and drive them out. *Never entertain anyone who claims to be a Christ, God, John the Baptist or such presumptive titles.*

Never allow divisions to take the word of persons claiming to represent Mr. Garvey or claiming to be sent by Mr. Garvey. *Let them produce the letter.* If they can't, drive them away. Wherever you find such fakers, hand them over to the police and make an example of them. Have it announced in the newspapers to scare others.

Whenever anyone is called upon to sit in a U.N.I.A. meeting and speak in your presence and say things not in keeping with the policy or membership training of the Association, after they have finished you should rise immediately and correct them, for the good of the membership. Instruct all presidents and presiding officers to do the same.

Whenever you think something is detrimental to the organization and its policies, never fail to correct it immediately, so that the people may not get the wrong impression. Always defend the organization and protect its name in the public press or otherwise. If you find an opportunity to debate with other people to maintain the principles of the organization, do so by challenging them. Before you debate, always read up on the point of view or subject, so as to be able to handle the same in keeping with the principles and objects of the U.N.I.A.

Whenever you are in doubt about anything in the U.N.I.A., write to headquarters. Never take it upon yourself to settle the question decisively if you are in doubt. Always say, "pending the ruling of my superior officers, this is my opinion" and leave it at that. Do this only when you are in doubt.

Encourage the divisions to use only programs at regular and public meetings that express the sentiments of Negroes. For instance, all recitations should be by Negro poets and authors. Songs, hymns and choruses should be by Negro composers, also.

Encourage the juveniles to study Negro poems and songs. Encourage local divisions to have a reader who is educated to read striking articles from the *Black Man* each week. Encourage some bright juvenile in each division to study and recite the "Tragedy of White Injustice." *Never have them recite this poem when white people are present.* Encourage some bright boy or girl to study and recite "African Fundamentalism."

Always keep these two major bits of literature before the people until they come to know them almost by heart.

Lesson 22

The Five-Year Plan of the U.N.I.A.

In 1934, at the International Convention of the U.N.I.A., held at Edelweiss Park, Cross Roads, St. Andrew, Jamaica, B.W.I., the President-General of the Association presented to the convention in session, the Five-Year Plan scheme, as the most possible and practical scheme through which the Association could rehabilitate itself, and carry out the major objects of the organization.

The scheme was thoroughly discussed and adopted by resolutions, properly moved and seconded and carried unanimously, as set out in the reprint circular from the *Black Man* Magazine, August-September, 1935, herewith incorporated. (Secure a copy of this circular).

Explanation of the Five-Year Plan

The Five-Year Plan is a scheme of colossal magnitude. Should the amount budgeted for be fully subscribed, it would enable the organization to, in a most practical and efficient manner, carry out, not only the industrial, commercial and other phases of the convention program, but to a great extent encourage and carry out many of the major objects for racial development. The idea is to get every Negro in the world to pledge to contribute voluntarily a sum of money for five years and pay the same within five years to the Plan.

The amount to be contributed is to be left entirely to the financial ability of the individual person. It was suggested that no person could be so poor as not to be able to contribute at least $5, within five years, to such a fund to assist in the general development of the race. Hence, nobody should be left out. The majority of people would be in a better position to contribute larger sums within the five years, for instance, some may be able to contribute $10, $20, $100, $500, or a $1,000 within five years.

There is every reason why every Negro should contribute to this fund voluntarily, for it would supply the organization with the financial resources to work without prejudice in the complete interest of the Race. It would help the organization realize all of its objects, from which each and every Negro would benefit.

The method of contributing to the fund is as follows: a person desirous of contributing makes a voluntary pledge for the amount to be contributed within five years, to be paid in installments, monthly, quarterly, semi-annually or annually, until paid. If possible, one could pay his pledge in one payment.

The pledge must be sent to the headquarters of the organization, the Parent Body, 2200 E. 40th Street, Cleveland, Ohio. The person pledging must give his or her full name, correct address and profession. The person may send the first installment with the pledge. On receipt of the first payment, a pledge card will be issued from headquarters to the subscriber or donor, with the amount pledged written on the card and the amount of the installment paid also entered.

The card is returned to the donor with the request that whenever other installments are to be paid that the card be forwarded with the installment for the amount to be entered on the card and in the ledger at headquarters and returned to the donor. After the pledge is fully paid, a certificate is issued by the Parent Body to show that the particular person paid the pledge in contributing to the Five Year Plan of the organization.

At the close of the five year period, a record will be published in which each donor who has paid up the pledge will have his or her name recorded for the information of all concerned.

The amount of money collected in the Plan will be appropriated for carrying out the many schemes authorized by the Convention of 1934, as set out in the circular referred to above. In explaining the Five-Year Plan, great stress must be laid on the fact that for the Negro to realize the objective of a nation and government of his own, he must first have financial security. While no individual person can create a nation or a government for the race, because each individual is looking after his own personal and private business, there must be an organized co-operative effort towards this end, hence, the effort is represented by the U.N.I.A. to which all Negroes must contribute and with which they must co-operate.

Established nations and governments get their revenue from taxes levied on the citizens. The Negro having no government cannot raise revenue for such a purpose in that way, hence, those who desire such a thing must be voluntary contributors.

The establishment of the different enterprises which will help to find employment for Negroes, and the profit of which will go to help the organization to carry out its nationalistic program, is in keeping with the principles of the organization; to hold all its properties and wealth in hereditary trust for the Negro Race. A contribution to the fund simply means that one is helping to place the race, through organization, in a position of financial security, through which it can march on to the realization of nationhood and government.

If everybody contributed just the amount of money that is thrown away on nonessentials, in five years, it would turn out that the very amount that would have been lost in waste, becomes the actual resource to establish that which is most needed by every Negro in the world.

Therefore, it is a patriotic duty of every Negro to contribute to the fund to make the Plan a success. The many enterprises we undertake in America, Canada, the West Indies, South and Central America and Africa, will be instrumental in finding employment for countless thousands of Negroes who never would have been employed otherwise; if the Plan is fully supported. The very magnitude of the Plan would give it status that would compel respect for the aims of the organization by all races. The Five-Year Plan has been seen as the most thoughtful economic scheme that could be undertaken as a solution to the economic, industrial, political and other problems of the Negro Race. No Negro should be left out of an interview on the subject without fully convincing him that he should contribute and to have him contribute to such a Plan.

How to Get Results

There is no use trying to represent the U.N.I.A. before making up your mind to get good results. The most important results are financial, active and moral support.

Financial support means to get as much money as possible to help finance the program. In getting such money, you must do so at the least cost, so that the amount received will produce a net that can be used for the purpose for which it was obtained.

Active results mean enrolling persons as active members of the Association; people who will always work as members to help put the program over.

Moral support means to secure sympathy and co-operation from individuals so that the organization can always count on such persons to do their best for the movement.

The Way to Get Money

There are many ways to get money for the U.N.I.A.
1. Approach and interview the most substantial members of the race in your community or your jurisdiction, such as, the ministers of the gospel, doctors, lawyers, business men and substantial tradesmen and persons of important occupations. Meet them at their homes or at their offices or places of business and seriously talk to them about the program of the organization. Explain to them all its details, aims and objects and after doing so, ask them to contribute to the assistance of the Association. Whatever they contribute must always be recorded with their names, occupations, and addresses. The names of such

persons must always be transmitted to the Parent Body for record, and all remarks that may be necessary to explain the character and disposition of the person must be added to the report on each person, so that the Parent Body can be advised as to the nature of the person to help the cause. This is important also, because communications with the people must be couched in language consistent with the person's disposition and intentions.

It must be taken for granted that people of this class will be sceptical at first, and have to be convinced by proper arguments. If you can win over the support of such people who are the natural representative class of the race in the community, you have achieved a great deal in winning the kind of support that will enable the organization to speak with authority because it has the best class of people supporting it.

2. In approaching ministers of the gospel, always be diplomatic enough to convince them of the Christian policy of the organization and the willingness of the organization to support the cause of the Christian religion. If the preacher is won over and he contributes, you may get further assistance from him by seeking permission to speak to his congregation to raise funds for the organization. In doing so, always arrange with him that a percentage of what is raised is given to the church, so that he may feel interested and satisfied to assist that way. No preacher should be left until he has consented to help in some way, because there is no greater way of the church showing its willingness to expand the functions of the church than by helping a cause like that of the U.N.I.A. If a preacher refuses, it is evident that he has not been in touch with the proper argument or that he is positively selfish.

One of the arguments to be used with the preacher is that by preaching unity, the Association is assisting the church by getting Negroes to support their own religion just as they are encouraged to support everything else that is theirs.

3. In approaching a doctor, you should point out that by the Association preaching unity, self-support and self-reliance, you are helping to increase his practice in the community. The same argument should be used for Negro lawyers and Negro business men.

4. The argument for those who are in good positions, employed as they may be by white people, is that the white people will not always employ Negroes. They will only do so until they have been approached or forced to substitute white employees for Negroes. You must convince these Negroes that the Association is seeking to establish such economic and industrial independence for the race as to be able to find substantial employment for its own men and women of quality and ability as evidenced by the program of the *Five-Year Plan*. Tell them that with the success their support will help bring about, this can be achieved.

5. A general approach should also be made to all other Negroes, in their homes, or at any place that you may conveniently meet them. Get them to contribute individually by using good sound arguments for their support.

6. The argument for the common people is, that there is no economic security for the race when it has to always depend on the white man's employment, therefore, by supporting the U.N.I.A. to the point of success, opportunities for employment will be created by the establishment of factories, mills, commercial, farming

and shipping enterprises, etc., which may offer them employment according to their training.

You can explain to all of them, professional and common people, alike, that contributing to the funds of the U.N.I.A. is no different to contributing to the funds of white organizations, which so many of them have done, for so many centuries, but the point is that while contributing to white organizations they are supplying the club to break their own heads, economically and politically. In contributing to the U.N.I.A., they will be supplying the ammunition that will be used to fight their enemies and to establish their own security. Explain to them that there is as much need for self-denial, even to the poorest person of the race, to help the U.N.I.A., as the self-denial to help other causes with which they are not directly identified.

There should be a proper method of approach in acquiring funds for the organization. If you are a representative of the organization, you will be supplied with the necessary credentials and the necessary account forms to submit for the gathering of such support. No one is supposed to make an appeal for the U.N.I.A. who is not authorized to do so, because it will mean trouble and fraud and would be unworthy of anyone who has secured these lessons. This method of approach must not be used for personal purposes, but only for the purposes of the U.N.I.A.

7. One of the major ways of raising funds for the U.N.I.A. is by public meetings advertised for the U.N.I.A. to explain its objects and to speak on its general program. Such meetings may be arranged through the agency of divisions of the Association or an affiliated one or through agents in a community. Where there is no branch of the Association, these meetings can be

arranged through friendly churches.

In organizing such meetings, an agent should be appointed first, a place secured and proper advertisement prepared and distributed in the community before the date of the meeting. In a community of 2,000 people, at least 1,000 handbills should be printed. In a community of 10,000 or more people, 2,000 or 3,000 handbills should be printed and widely distributed among the Negro population. All agents should be written to and asked to see that this is carried out so that upon going to the place to address the meeting, you will not go where no one knows about it. Always word your handbills in the most attractive manner so as to create general interest among Negroes.

You should mention that you are a graduate of the School of African Philosophy to suggest to the public that you have rare, uncommon knowledge of great importance. This will attract their curiosity. When speaking at such a meeting you should be at your best on the subject that you are going to discuss. After you have made your speech, sit down for a couple of minutes, then rise again and make your financial appeal.

Unless you are addressing a division, don't make an appeal for money in the speech that you make, because people will think that you are only speaking for money. Immediately after the speech, get up and make another short speech for funds to support the organization.

Always have your meeting well organized inside by arranging for ushers to take up the collection after you have asked for special contributions, which should be brought up to a table immediately in front of the platform. After you have made the appeal for special contributions of large amounts, then get the ushers to take up the small contributions. Never ask for extraordinary amounts in special contributions. Consider the pockets of the people. You may ask for $5, $3, $2 or $1 from those who can give that much for such a cause; then after you have exhausted that, you may even ask for special contributions of 50¢ and then take up a collection from those who may not be able to give more than 25¢ or 10¢.

When you go into a strange community where the people are not members of the U.N.I.A., make your first public meeting a meeting for obtaining members. All members who are to join must pay $1; 35¢ of which is the dues for the 1st month, 25¢ is the joining fee, 25¢ is for the constitution and 15¢ is for the button and certificate. Each person must be given a receipt for the $1, then the person's name, occupation, address and age is registered in the book.

If you have secured seven or more people as members, you have enough to start a division. After the meeting, call upon those who have joined to appoint a president, and then have them elect a vice-president, a treasurer and a secretary.

Leave a constitution and tell them that they must control the organization in keeping with the constitution. Tell them that they will be privileged to hold regular meetings; suggest twice a week, but particularly on Sunday at 3 P.M. or at 8 P.M. Instruct them to work to secure more members and then they can apply to the Parent Body for a charter, the cost of which is $25. Also tell them that they are privileged to collect money in their community from others who are sympathetic to the Association to secure money for the charter.

You should keep in constant touch with the secretary you have elected and find out when they are ready to apply for their charter, then recommend that they contact the Parent Body for the charter. When they receive their charter, they should be advised to have a special meeting for the dedication of the charter. Then invite all the Negroes of the community to attend at which time they should try to get more members for the Association.

If you remain in town the second night, call for members also and make an appeal for funds for the Association. Always see that you secure your expenses and have money as a net to forward to the Parent Body whom you represent. If you remain in town for one, two or three days to work up a division or to visit a division, you should take the time to interview all the potential members in the community, to get financial support for the organization, so that the expenses of the trip will not only be on the meeting but on the community from whom you may get financial support.

In getting people to join a division and elect officers, you should leave with them that portion of the first month's dues that is the division's, according to the constitutional law. Also leave them a portion of the proceeds to enable them to start out with something in their treasury.

When setting up a new division, you should always advise them to rent a hall of their own where they will be able to hold their meetings without being disturbed. Suggest to them that they should not only depend on the regular monthly dues and the collections to support the division, but they should organize entertainment of an innocent nature, such as, dances, concerts, beauty contests, popularity contests, or any kind of social event on a regular basis to help bear the cost of the rental of the place. You should explain to them that from the very beginning, the division must make a regular monthly report to the Parent Body; this is in accordance with the constitution.

You should point out to them and then mark those important sections of the constitution that deal with the relationship between a division and the Parent Body. If you are a representative of the U.N.I.A. with credentials, such as a commissioner of a state, you should raise funds in the following ways for the Parent Body which you represent: 1. Hold bazaars within the state, 2. picnics, 3. garden parties, 4. concerts, 5. or any general amusement that the public is accustomed to, and would likely patronize for a cause. 6. Flower days, Rose days, tag days or self-denial days. If these functions are to take in the entire state, then ask all friends or divisions within the state to co-operate. When these events are held within a special community, then ask all friends or divisions in that particular community to co-operate. This must only be done with previous arrangements with the Parent Body. A report to the Parent Body must accompany every such function. All these functions must be held in the name of the organization. You may also have groups of people in your jurisdiction organize house parties and give public entertainment for the benefit of the organization. A way to do this is to approach some responsible person on a street or in a neighborhood and ask him to invite his friends to his house for the party. If possible, you should always be present, unless the person you have asked to have the party is a responsible and honest person, who is in sympathy with the organization.

If you arrange a tag day or a flower day, this should be of a private organizational nature, because if made public, it would be in conflict with certain municipal or state laws governing charities. These things are to be organized within the organization and among its friends. You can appoint members of the organization, such as units of the Black Cross Nurses, to go into people's homes and offices and ask them to buy a tag or a flower to help the cause. Do not have them do it publicly, on the street, except in communities where you are privileged to do so.

In organizing these things, always try to get interesting people to help who will take part in these activities for the love of the cause and not for payment. You can arrange with churches in your jurisdiction to stage plays at their church hall or in the church on a percentage basis, and then get local talent in your jurisdiction to contribute to the program free of cost. In this way you will find yourself continuously active. After you have done this thoroughly for a year, you will become acquainted with all the parties and it will then be very easy for you to do the same thing annually.

In such work, let every minute count, because if you appreciate all this, you will have no time for idleness. As far as white people are concerned, we do not specialize in seeking contributions from them, but where you think it is wise to arrange lectures among them, revealing only the humanitarian part of the work, you may conduct such lectures and raise a collection or ask for help only on those humanitarian grounds. Do not commit yourself in any statement that would lead them to think that they could become members of your Association, or be affiliated with it or have any part in it. To do so, would be a direct violation of the constitution and against the Association. This applies to individuals of the other races that you may ask to contribute to any special fund, but wherever such contributions have been made, a record should be kept of the person's name and address, and a report should be given to headquarters, with remarks made to show the contributor's race, for the purpose of guiding the Parent Body in communications with such persons, then and in the future.

School of African Philosophy
College Yell

1. We must win, we shall win, we will win!

Chorus

Win, yes win, and win to win!

2. You and I shall win to win

   For Africa, for Africa we win,

   We must win, we shall win, we will win!

United Chorus

Win, yes win, and win to win!

For Africa, for Africa, we'll win to win!

The Creed of Goodness

To pass the time in doing good,
To count the evils we put down,
To have our deeds so understood,
Is nobler than to wear a crown,
To bless the people as we go,
To scatter seeds that grow to life,
To strike all sin a deadly blow,
Is better than to stir up strife.

For this of all, is greatest fame,
That none on earth can e'er destroy.

By Marcus Garvey

NOTES (Editor's)

1. This, Garvey's longest poem, is reprinted in Tony Martin, ed., *The Poetical Works of Marcus Garvey* (Dover, Mass.: The Majority Press, 1983). It was originally published in pamphlet form (New York, 1927) by Mrs. Amy Jacques Garvey, while her husband was incarcerated in the United States.

2. This is a paraphrase of a line from "Rule Britannia," a patriotic song sung throughout the Black (and white) portions of the British empire.

3. Garvey seems to be referring here to an incident which took place in Cardiff in 1919, rather than in 1923. See Tony Martin, *The Pan-African Connection* (Dover, Mass.: The Majority Press, 1984), p. 51.

4. Amy Jacques Garvey, ed., *The Philosophy and Opinions of Marcus Garvey,* originally published in two volumes in New York in 1923 and 1925. (Reprint. London: Frank Cass, 1967 and New York: Atheneum, 1969), II pp. 69-71.

5. The original manuscript says 1917, an obvious mistake, probably typographical.

6. The original manuscript says 148th Street, an obvious mistake.

Index

Books from The Majority Press